the

LOVE

compatibility

book

the
LOVE
compatibility
book

THE 12 PERSONALITY TRAITS THAT CAN LEAD YOU TO YOUR SOULMATE

EDWARD HOFFMAN, PH.D. &
MARCELLA BAKUR WEINER, PH.D.

NEW WORLD LIBRARY
NOVATO, CALIFORNIA

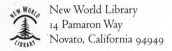

New World Library
14 Pamaron Way
Novato, California 94949

Text design and typography by Tona Pearce Myers
Cover design by Mary Beth Salmon

The purpose of this book is solely to help readers understand relationships today from the perspective of personality assessment. The sample test items and scoring interpretations provided are not intended in any way to provide actual diagnostic, clinical, or therapeutic guidance for anyone who may read this book. Those who are experiencing emotional difficulties, whether from a relationship or otherwise, are advised to see a licensed mental health professional immediately for accurate diagnosis and intervention.

Library of Congress Cataloging-in-Publication Data
Weiner, Marcella Bakur
  The love compatibility book / by Marcella Bakur Weiner and Edward Hoffman.
    p.   cm.
Includes index.
  ISBN 1-57731-226-0 (pbk. : alk. paper)
  1. Love. 2. Intimacy (Psychology) 3. Mate selection. I. Hoffman, Edward II. Title.
  HQ801 .W6349 2003
  646.7'7—dc21   2002151203

First Printing, January 2003
ISBN 1-57731-226-0
Printed in Canada on acid-free, partially recycled paper
Distributed to the trade by Publishers Group West

10 9 8 7 6 5 4 3 2 1

To Elaine,
who has taught me that love is bigger than I thought

— Dr. Edward Hoffman

To my husband, Wilhelm,
who is love compatibility in action: my eternal gratitude

— Dr. Marcella Bakur Weiner

Anything, everything, little or big becomes an adventure
when the right person shares it.
Nothing, nothing, nothing is worthwhile
when we have to do it alone.

— Kathleen Norris, *Hands Full of Living*

CONTENTS

ACKNOWLEDGMENTS

In conceptualizing and writing this book with Marcella Bakur Weiner, I wish to thank editorial director Georgia Hughes at New World Library for her initial and sustained enthusiasm throughout the project. Katie Farnam Conolly and Mimi Kusch ably guided the manuscript through production. Over the years, I've enjoyed many stimulating discussions with Fannie Cheng, Dr. Steven Joseph, Dr. Ted Mann, Dr. Sam Menahem, Paul Palnik, Dr. Russ Reeves, and K. Dean Stanton on psychological topics central to this book. These dialogues have been a continuing source of inspiration to me. My international colleagues Dr. Xu Jinsheng in China and Drs. Naoki Nomura, Shoji Muramoto, and Yoshikazu Ueda in Japan have enhanced my appreciation for cross-cultural issues in social science. As research assistants, Juliana Bouval, Harvey Gitlin, and

Linda Joyce have been eager and efficient. On the home front, I wish to thank my family for its sustained support in my clinical work and writing.

— Edward Hoffman

My deep appreciation to editorial director Georgia Hughes and her responsive staff for their support and generosity of time above and beyond the call of duty. Katie Farnam Conolly and Mimi Kusch gave tirelessly of their time and talents. My deep appreciation to them. To my colleagues and research teammates, Drs. Robert Plutchik and Hope Conte, I am deeply indebted. Dr. Jeanne Teresi, a statistical whiz, and her staff, in particular Joseph Eimicka, have my heartfelt gratitude. Thanks to Joyce Finks for her generosity with her computer skills. To Gloria Stevens, who meticulously distributed and collected our surveys, thanks for a superb job. And to my colleagues at Marymount Manhattan College, Drs. Richard Tietze, Cheryl Paradis, and Linda Solomon, your efforts are appreciated. To friends Colette and Rosemarie Antonelli, who dispersed Q forms during a party, many thanks. And to colleague and longtime friend Dr. Aaron Lieberman, who took time from his university classes to assist our collecting of data, we are beholden. To my family, who are consistently there for me, I extend my deep-felt love.

— Marcella Bakur Weiner

INTRODUCTION

This book has been a long time germinating: For the past seven years, we've been steadily developing a new theoretical model and a powerful set of tools for enhancing love relationships. It emerged from our intense dissatisfaction as licensed psychologists with the standard approach to couples counseling. Although we had dutifully studied and practiced it since earning our respective doctorates, it had proven virtually useless in the "real world." From our combined experience, almost nobody seemed to be benefiting: neither in our busy New York City offices nor in the wider domain of intimacy study and treatment. There *had* to be a better way.

Reflecting our training in survey research and personality testing, we were sure that a more effective approach to intimacy could be forged empirically. And, at the outset, we wanted it to be humanistic and spiritually oriented rather than reductionist and mechanistic. Indeed, a key motivator for creating our new model lay in our disappointment with the "one-size-fits-all" conception of love relationships. Since both of us are involved parents and family members — not just clinicians — we could clearly see that different kinds of people generate different types of intimacy, each with its particular strengths, weaknesses, and dynamics.

For example, couples consisting of two musicians, two teachers, or two accountants exhibited undeniably different patterns than those in which the romantic partners have widely disparate occupations. While having similar careers or similar interests — such as enjoying loud parties or art galleries, caring for pets, skiing, wearing chic clothing, or indulging in exotic travels — alone certainly didn't predict happiness among the couples we studied, personality compatibility increasingly presented the key to lasting harmony.

As our work progressed in the late 1990s, we incorporated the latest findings from biological and developmental psychology, especially the study of temperament. Ever more clearly, we saw that our approach was not only exciting in theoretical terms but eminently applicable too. That is, we had evolved a method by which people could objectively assess their relationship based on the twelve "core personality" traits affecting intimacy and thereby make appropriate choices and plans. What finally lay in our hands was a truly innovative, scientifically grounded, and blame-free method for understanding love relationships: a method that could truly make a difference in the daily lives of nearly all.

We had both written many books before. But for this one, we were initially hesitant to swim against the professional tide and publicize our approach. Nevertheless, after repeated encouragement from colleagues and friends, we decided to undertake this project. The task has been most enjoyable. Over the past year and a half, we've spoken to countless people about our viewpoint and method and gained a great deal of satisfaction. More than 200 men and women completed our surveys.

Working together as both psychologists and writers has also been immensely rewarding and has fortified our conviction that maximum compatibility on the "Big 12," as we call them, is a powerful force for synergy in many endeavors. *The Love Compatibility Book* has been an exciting accomplishment for us. If it helps you to understand yourself and your partner better in the quest for soulmate bliss, we will have fulfilled our purpose in authorship.

PART ONE

WHAT REALLY MATTERS

CHAPTER ONE

THE SEARCH
FOR INTIMACY

The search for intimacy is now a worldwide phenomenon beginning earlier in our lives than ever before and lasting into our seventies, eighties, and beyond. For the adventurous, becoming romantically involved with someone five hundred or five thousand miles away is now as easy as a click on your Internet browser. The goal? To find and keep your romantic ideal, of course. While there's certainly nothing wrong with this intent, people can waste so much time and effort because they lack a beacon. It's like groping in a dark tunnel.

We now offer the beacon to make your search infinitely easier, more effective, and relevant to who *you* are. This beacon is the product of our combined forty years of clinical experience and research in personality and developmental psychology, not of traditional marriage/couples counseling based on obsolete views and myths about love. We offer not only a revolutionary new perspective, but also a viable method and a complete set of tools for your use. Indeed, over the past seven years, we have found our method to work again and again. Finally, our colleagues and friends persuaded us to write this book.

Finding someone who is compatible takes considerable time and energy, and it is often discouraging. What if we told you that our method, based on scientific research, eliminates all the frustrating guesswork and leads you decisively to your likely soulmate — not a fantasy, generic Prince Charming or Aphrodite? Even though people are using many innovative methods in their search for a mate, such as surfing the Internet, they are unknowingly using a love-model that is obsolete — much like a pilot using an archaic flight map. Why is it obsolete? Because of pervasive myths, which though outdated and invalid, are still accepted by most. Basically they hinge on the outworn concept that everybody is alike in their intimacy needs, and therefore all we need in selecting a love partner is attractiveness and kindness, and that all possible differences will eventually work out. To believe this now is as sensible as believing that the sun revolves around the earth.

To forge ahead in your quest for lasting love, you need to know the essence of your core personality and that of the one you choose. When this knowledge is lacking, the following example may reflect your experience. A young woman who describes herself as "sensual and loving" stated that she had had forty dates in a few short months, no doubt squeezed into a busy work schedule almost as an afterthought. As is true of many, she rarely got to a second date with the same person. Said one woman with similar "hyperdating" experiences, "It just wasn't what I'd hoped for. The disappointments seemed to stack up." The underlying reason is plainly stated by one young man, "There is the notion that somehow mates are interchangeable, like parts in a car." He adds, "If I fantasize, my ideal mate will be wrapped in misty perfection. But, in truth, people don't come that way." Indeed!

While a boon to many, the Internet definitely has its romantic limitations. Says one young woman about someone she met on-line, "Ian was so great; we had conversations that just flowed, hours at a time that seemed like seconds. And then we met. And I thought, 'My God, is this the same person? How could this be?' And the photo he sent? I think the photographer was looking in someone else's direction." The answer isn't necessarily to stop using technology, but to replace our obsolete view of intimacy. Contrary to the outmoded cliché that "ignorance is bliss," the price of ignorance has in fact never been higher.

A SHORT HISTORY OF LOVE

If the search for intimacy is as old as humanity, how did it all begin? According to the Bible, "God created Adam in His image, male and female in one body, and God created them male and female. On the day when God created them, God blessed them and called their name Adam" (Genesis 5:2). God, in his love, saw that Adam was alone and needed a mate. So he fashioned Eve, which in Hebrew means "mother of all life," from Adam's rib. And then, as we all know, along came the testing serpent. While some regard God's banishment of Adam and Eve from the garden as the "Fall," others see it not as punitive but as a way of plunging them into a new world so that they could know love for one another and for God.

Adam heard God: "Adam does not have a partner that fits" (Genesis 2:21–24). Everybody needs a partner who fits, but not everybody has one fashioned from one of their body parts! In reality, the relationship that works is not one in which we're attached at the hip but one in which our chosen partner mirrors who we are. With the right person, our passion climbs to dizzying heights, pushing past our preconceived notions of ourselves so that we are both most outside ourselves while at the same time, paradoxically, most inside.

Adam and Eve knew sexual love, which was also a sacred love, including God. Sacred love, as true today as it was then, always involves an Energy, a Light, a way of being the most present to ourselves. Says the thirteenth-century *Book of Splendor*, a sacred text of Jewish mysticism: "No other kiss is like the ecstasy of the moment when spirit cleaves to spirit in a kiss" (Zohar 2:146a). A verse from the biblical Song of Songs (4:10–11) says it beautifully:

> *How much better is thy love than wine*
> *And the smell of thine ointment than all spices*
> *Thy lips, O my spouse drop as the honeycomb*
> *honey and milk are under thy tongue*

The ancient Egyptians, 3,500 years ago, were the first to write love poems. Using metaphors, they compared love to an illness that only the presence of the beloved could cure in a sweet entrapment. For the Egyptians, like for many cultures, the heart was the organ of love, an inner structure apart from the rest of the personality. Some poems concentrate on the lover's own heart:

My heart flutters hastily,
When I think of my love of you:
It lets me not act sensibly.

The early Greeks, focusing on sexual passion, asserted that the reason we choose one person over another to be our beloved cannot be consciously known. But it was Plato, one of the greatest Western philosophers of Western culture — his school, known simply as the "Academy," was the first intellectual center in Europe — who recognized in the fifth century B.C.E. that love is based on a longing, on a wish for union to release us from our lonely existence. He believed that in love, one person and one person only can offer us this bliss.

The twelfth century saw the flourishing of "courtly love," its chief spokespeople being the troubadours, or poet-musicians, and their chief tenet being the ennobling power of love. In their captivating vision, love is a burning passion. Rarely extinguished, it was not deemed possible between husband and wife, though fidelity was pledged between lovers while love lasted. Sang one troubadour: "By nothing is man made so worthy as by love and the courting of women, for thence arise delight and song and all that pertains to excellence. No man is of value without love."[1] Men, they believed, are crude and insensitive until love strikes them, and then they acquire courtesy, a thirst for learning, and gentleness of manner. Analogous to this viewpoint are those

---

1   Martin S. Bergmann, *The Anatomy of Loving: The Story of Man's Quest to Know What Love Is* (New York: Columbia University Press, 1987).

found in some early Church writings, which, in honoring the Celestial Mother, state: "The heart has its own reasons, which the intellect does not know."

But perhaps no historical period has produced such a profusion of discourses on love as the first half of the seventeenth century. For example, in a painting by Titian, a goddess is gazing into a mirror held up to her by Cupid. The clear message is that self-love is a valid form of love. As she gazes at herself, she contemplates, a moving inward into the deepest regions of the self, not a mere looking into her mirror image for affirmation of her outer beauty.

We lose this self-focus after the early stage of babyhood when, omnipotent in this new world we've entered, we are not yet aware of human limitations. Happily for most of us, this form of early self-love shifts into an adult form in which we are able to observe the real qualities of a potential lover, and, most significant, to evaluate the future of the relationship. Blinders off, we now progress from the dream state to one of experiencing our relationship as *real*. Bliss, however, remains. Says the eighteenth-century German philosopher Arthur Schopenhauer, who was much influenced by the Eastern philosophies, especially early Hinduism and Buddhism: "Love is endless bliss associated with the possession of one particular person and unthinkable pain at the thought that the possession is unattainable. I encounter millions of bodies in my life. Of those millions, I desire some hundreds, but of the hundreds I love only one."[2]

Such romantic writings certainly tug at the heart. But the reality is that many people find themselves in unhappy

---

2   T. Sarthes, "Ambivalence, Passion, and Love," *Journal of American Psycho-analytic Association* 25 (1977): 53.

relationships. They have the desire for intimacy, but not the tools. The quest for intimacy becomes a hit-or-miss affair, with much wasted time and energy and many disappointments along the way. If the desire for enduring intimacy is so prevalent, why aren't more people finding it? What, indeed, is intimacy? How can it be defined? Yes, physical chemistry is a necessary component, but even more relevant is the realm of personalities and compatibility between them.

SOME MYTHS ABOUT LOVE

Basically, lasting intimacy is based on personality compatibility. And in this regard, two conditions are absolutely necessary: 1) you must know your own "core personality" as it relates to intimacy; 2) you must then match it up with an appropriate partner, someone who is romantically available and similarly interested in finding romantic love. Among the most pernicious barriers to achieving compatibility is the prevalence of long-standing myths surrounding romantic love. Of these, we have identified four. Let's examine each in turn.

MYTH ONE: ONE SIZE FITS ALL

This myth suggests that people are more or less the same when it comes to their intimacy needs. Many believe that somehow a generic Prince Charming or Aphrodite will be sent to them and that love will be like a sweet elixir to intoxicate and provide a lifetime of bliss. Others think more of the concept of mother-infant love, that a relationship will be like a mother holding her newborn to her breast, each enveloped in that early stage of oneness when the world is perfect, heaven on earth. But even here, all mothers and children are different. One mother prefers to nurse, while another thinks it's old-fashioned. And if mothers are different, so too are infants, right at birth. Ask any parent with more than one child, and he or she will tell you that no two are alike. If your fingerprints are unique, God given to you and you alone, how can your intimacy needs be exactly the same as those of other people? They cannot. To know what you need from someone, you first must know yourself. If we are all different from one another, so too are our responses to life. You are not one kind of person one day and totally different the next. The point is to know who *you* are, regardless of circumstances.

MYTH TWO: IF YOU WORK ON YOUR RELATIONSHIP, ALL WILL BE WELL

A common view, perpetuated by movies, TV, books, and therapists is that a relationship is something you have to work on. This is a huge fallacy! Far more accurate is the view of the ancient Greek philosophers who said that leisure is something you enjoy for itself, with turning inward being its highest form, while work, if it is enjoyable and something you look forward to, is leisure.

A relationship that is all work fills you with the same kind of tightness in your stomach as a job you truly dislike — a job that gives you headaches or ulcers and makes you ache to have the day end. Your partner is not someone to be "worked on" like a car — to be shined, washed, and tinkered with — but a person sent to you as a means of teaching you lessons about yourself, a true gift from God. The result is that you grow from this blessed experience, but only if this individual is helping you to move deeper within yourself — the best haven that you have. Think of a plant. It only needs to receive the right amount of water and sunshine. It doesn't *work* at growing. Nor should you.

If your partner can match your "watering" needs, you're in luck. If he or she can't, then you have a clear message. Staying in a relationship past its prime, with work as its main focus, is stressful. Friends and others may tell you to keep working at it, but a better way to help things along is to move into yourself. Learn to listen to your body, to your breath, to your feelings. Be in tune with the sacred found within. The answers will come to you. The concept of "work," too often a false idol, can make us overlook the sacredness of life and love, which is what a relationship is all about!

MYTH THREE: LOVE CONQUERS ALL

While this myth is firmly believed by many, it is obvious from our growing global divorce rate that love alone is not enough. Indeed, psychological studies have shown that significant differences between people supersede love and bring unhappiness. Still, this concept clings to us like flies to honey. Women, in particular, are susceptible to it. Says Jennifer: "Alex had been a lonely child. His parents were both hard-working professionals whom he seldom saw. Rather, nannies came and went. An only child, he was placed in nursery school even before the age of acceptance, his parents' persuasion working on the administrator. When we dated for a while, one day I asked Alex what he had wanted to be when a boy. He answered, 'A patient. That's who my parents saw all day long, and I thought, If only I could be one of them.'"

Jennifer wiped her eyes as she spoke, evidently still moved by the telling. She went on: "We married. Alex was hard to live with, but I thought I loved him so I'd just hang in. Everyone said it was the right thing to do, and I didn't want to abandon him like it seemed his parents had. I just kept thinking, I'll love

the **LOVE** compatibility book

him with all my heart and soul. And he was a good man; we both went to church, though I felt I was the more committed one. The problem? Alex was seldom available to me. Always busy, he seemed to be constantly tinkering. Not much was really broken, but there he was fixing the car, the computer, or going to friends to help them with fixing ... whatever. One time we were invited to a Halloween party. Alex asked me how I would dress. I said, hoping he would catch on: 'As a computer.' 'Why?' he asked. 'Because,' I said, 'maybe then you'll pay attention to me.' He just shrugged, shot me a sarcastic look, and went off to fix something. We finally split. I had run out of love."

As an emotion, love encompasses joy, acceptance, receiving, and attaining. It is the opposite of sadness, which is based on the loss of a valued attachment or on deprivation. Still, while love is an emotion, it is deeply connected to personality. When a person's emotional state persists over time or is frequently repeated, we say that he or she has a particular personality *trait*. For example, if someone is angry much of the time, we label that individual as quarrelsome and tend to stay away from her. Conversely, if someone is loving, we experience him as caring and nurturing, one of the twelve core traits we highlight in the next chapter. And our movement is forward, for companionship is a joyous experience.

Traits are seen in children early on and stay constant throughout life. In fact, the older we become, the more entrenched our traits become. An onion becomes a bigger onion, a carrot a bigger carrot, but a carrot never becomes an onion, and vice versa. While this notion is undisputed today, it has not always been accepted. Had this viewpoint been emphasized just a few decades ago, it would have been regarded as completely alien. Children were born, moldable as clay; they could be pushed or pulled into any shape the parents wished. All the parents needed to know was what they wanted of their child, and it could be achieved.

Evan was a quiet child, loving to read and enjoying solitude. His dad was convinced that "Evan could do better. Something must be wrong with him." A concerned parent, he said, "Son, get out there and talk to people. Get to know them. Then, maybe later on, you can be a salesman, in charge of a whole department, just like me. You could be a big success." Were Evan to follow that route, which would be foreign to his nature, the road ahead, as you could predict, would be a disaster.

The same was true for Natasha, who wanted to be a dancer. Early on, when she was an infant, when people held her, they remarked that she seemed to dance in their arms. Her parents were appalled when Natasha, at age five, stated most clearly that, indeed, she did want to be a dancer. Said her mother, "Natasha, dancers have a short life. We are no longer in Russia, and you cannot be a ballerina. Even here in America, it's not a real career. Be a teacher, like me." Fortunately, for Natasha, she went her own way. And, last we heard, she is still dancing professionally, in her thirties, and with noted recognition. As a bonus, she has also found her true love, a male dancer with whom she shares much besides their love of music and dancing.

MYTH FOUR: OPPOSITES ATTRACT

The silly notion that opposites attract came to the fore after World War II when social scientists were, for the first time, probing who was marrying whom. Curiously, while most researchers found that individuals largely tended to marry based on such factors as age, religion, socioeconomic status, and education, sociologist Robert F. Winch disagreed. His theory suggested that we are attracted to those whose needs conversely match our own. Thus, he said, dominant and submissive people are paradoxically drawn to each other. This view was later simply called the "Opposites Attract" theory. His research methodology, however, was strongly criticized, the overwhelming majority of researchers obtaining results contrary to his findings. Though still popular, Winch's conception is totally obsolete. It works for electricity, but not for people.

We come into this world with our own minds, hearts, and spirits. Coming from diverse genetic backgrounds, we are fully equipped with our own tastes, feelings, wants, and needs. And our primary built-in desire is to see these fulfilled. We are essentially who we are, and will remain so. Just as the sun is always the sun, we are constant in our beingness. To be recognized for who we are, we need someone who not only understands us but who can share with us. Even the sun and moon, while seemingly different, are not. What they have in common is light. The sun has dominance during the day, the moon during the night, an equal and eternal trade-off. Not truly opposites, each emanates its own form of brilliance, their commonality.

It has been our experience in decades of counseling practice that every couple must have something in common for lasting intimacy to be possible. So why has this myth persisted with such vigor? Perhaps when we meet someone who is so different from us we think, "Ah, but I can change him to be more like me." Perhaps we are drawn to this kind of challenge. But chances are this person will stay exactly as he was meant to be — himself. Change, as we know, comes only from the inside.

To help you find someone with whom you are truly compatible, we offer you a revolutionary way of searching. Based on scientific research and yet humanistic and spiritual, it provides a path for you to find not a fantasy, but a real person who has qualities that are the "best fit" for you and you alone. The foundation of our system is that, first and foremost, you must know yourself. This is what Mechthild of Magdeburg, a thirteenth-century poet said:

> *A fish cannot drown in water*
> *A bird does not fall in air.*
> *In the fire of creation,*
> *Gold does not vanish;*
> *The fire brightens,*
> *Each creature God made*
> *Must live in its own true nature;*
> *How can I resist my nature,*
> *That lives for oneness with God?*[3]

It is our hope that this book will help you discover your own nature so deeply that you'll know exactly your soulmate's qualities. Yes, soulmates *do* exist — and you can find yours. Are you ready to start looking effectively? Let's move on now to the specifics!

How to Use This Book

This book is intended as a practical guide for leading you to your soulmate. Chapters 2 and 3 provide the framework for our exciting new approach. Then chapters 4 through 15 specifically highlight each of the Big 12 traits. Through our descriptions,

---

3 Stephen Mitchell, ed., *The Enlightened Heart: An Anthology of Sacred Poetry* (New York: Harper & Row, 1989), 64.

including early signs of development and popular stereotypes — and revealing, scientifically validated self-quizzes — you'll gain the ability to know yourself and your partner. On each of the Big 12, you'll be presented with a short quiz designed to reveal your true nature. Based on your answers, you'll get a score placing you either high or low on the particular trait. Thus, you'll be able to see objectively how you match up — and ultimately to rate your overall romantic compatibility. Presented in chapter 16, this process involves two simple steps: calculating your individualized Intimacy Profile and then your Compatibility Profile as a couple. Finally, chapter 17 and the conclusion will place the results in a meaningful context for action.

If you're currently single, the self-quizzes and resulting Intimacy Profile you construct will be tremendously helpful in guiding your search. Thus, whether you're single or with a partner, you'll be empowered to make the right choice for lasting intimacy. You'll clearly see what actual qualities your soulmate possesses — based entirely on who you are. For only by being yourself in the deepest way can the blessed gift of enduring love be yours.

CHAPTER TWO

ROMANTIC

COMPATIBILITY

INTRODUCING THE BIG 12

D o you know what you want in a love partner? Or do you expect that you'll "just feel it's right" when the time comes? Have you always believed this? If you could right now magically conjure up your ideal partner, what personal qualities would she or he possess? On the subject of romantic love, would you call yourself idealistic, cynical, or somewhere in between? Few subjects today excite us more than love and intimacy — and not only in the United States, but increasingly around the world as well. In an era of unprecedented life-longevity, health, and education, men and women as never before are seeking romantic intimacy as a source of happiness. But what exactly is intimacy in love?

What you have probably heard is true: What matters most is companionship. As countless research studies and counseling room conversations bear out, *a companion is someone who shares your most important traits relating to intimacy.* And to find that companion — your soulmate — you must first know your own intimacy needs and traits. Then you can find that special compatible one.

Maybe you're asking, Are people really that different? The answer is — absolutely yes. Our own sample research data with regard to intimacy, encompassing more than two hundred adults from diverse backgrounds, confirms this. Some people adore boisterous parties, while others detest them. Some proclaim that their sexuality is a basic part of who they are, whereas others utterly reject that view. Some strive to live the Golden Rule — "Do unto others as you would have them do unto you" — yet others dismiss it as a prescription only for suckers and for getting hurt.

Do you enjoy lots of activity? Or do you prefer to lounge during your weekends and leisure hours? Do you like to do things on impulse, or do you plan everything carefully? For example, does planning your vacation carefully make you feel content or confined? Do you prefer being around people who are typically calm or rather emotionally intense?

We cannot say it more concisely: The better you know your own core personality, the swifter you'll find the right partner. Specifically, this involves appraising yourself honestly on the key traits that underline all intimacy — developing what we call your Intimacy Profile (which we will do in chapter 16). For over and over again, we have found that lasting intimacy is based eminently on compatibility.

How early in life do these qualities form? It may surprise you to learn that even babies differ widely on such characteristics as extroversion or shyness, activity level, emotional intensity, adaptability to change, desire for stroking and touching, and responsiveness to bright colors or music.

The field of biological temperament, as it's known, has increasingly shown that we retain and sharpen these personality differences as we grow into adulthood. In fact, the older we get, the more we become who we inherently are as unique, God-given individuals. To put it simply, if Paul at age three adores listening to music, it's probable he'll do so at age thirteen or thirty-three. If five-year-old Kayla already enjoys a reputation as a terrific social butterfly, she's more likely than her peers are to become president of her high school council and to go onto a political career.

So if these core traits manifest early, how easily can we change them? The answer is, hardly at all. By the time nearly all of us have reached early adolescence — and quite possibly several years before that — our essential personality is well formed and increasingly solidifies as the years pass. The social phenomenon of the high school or college reunion speaks powerfully to this point: What nearly everyone notices, often to their utter amazement, is how little their classmates have really changed despite their occupations, geographic locations, or income levels. Decades later, Jennifer and Steve are, emotionally, exactly how you remember them in ninth-grade homeroom or college sophomore year.

Certainly it's possible to modify our personality to some extent. The entire fields of psychotherapy and counseling are predicated on the view that we can alter our attitudes, behavioral tendencies, and goals in life. But psychologists also know that that it becomes harder for us to change our personalities as we get older. And, when change does occur, it's almost always a modification, rather than a huge alteration, of our inner "core."

The goal in counseling and psychotherapy, therefore, is to help the individual function better in terms of *who he or she is* rather than trying to effect a total "makeover." So if Kelly feels lonely and is basically a shy person, she won't be expected to dominate boisterous parties as a result of guidance. Rather, the emphasis will be on helping Kelly create friendships through quiet, one-on-one or small-group gatherings consistent with who she is.

How many traits really matter in the forging of intimacy? After seven years of developing our approach based on couples therapy and research, we have decisively uncovered twelve that vitally affect all romantic relationships, that either make or break intimacy. This precise number is important, and it has been determined both clinically and scientifically. Throughout this book and our professional work, we have affectionately dubbed these traits as the "Big 12."

THE BIG 12 TRAITS AFFECTING INTIMACY

Here is a list of these core traits, along with descriptions of each.

1. *Need for Companionship.* Do you get lonely easily? Is it important for your daily well-being to have heart-to-heart conversations, in which you share your desires and hopes, disappointments and dreams? Or do you prefer maintaining your privacy and keeping others at an emotional distance?

2. *Idealism.* How idealistic are you? Do you believe that people are basically good and trustworthy and that following the Golden Rule ("Do onto others as they would do onto you.") is the best way to live? Do you believe in a Higher Power that guides us? Or

do you believe that people are inherently dishonest and untrustworthy and that human existence is essentially "dog-eat-dog"? We have found this trait to be the single most important element of compatibility and have labeled its opposite as pragmatism.

3. *Emotional Intensity.* Do you cry easily at movies? Do you often enjoy belly laughs? Are your feelings strong about most people and situations? Or are you emotionally low-key and placid, with little in everyday life evoking much inner heat?

4. *Spontaneity.* Do you typically act on impulse? Do you prefer making spur-of-the-moment decisions and keeping your schedule as open as possible? Or do you like to plan things well ahead and keep to an established routine? To put it plainly, do you enjoy vacations in which every day is carefully planned in advance, or does that make you feel straitjacketed?

5. *Libido.* Are frequent touching and sex important to your well-being? Do you enjoy erotic movies, pictures, and jokes? Or do you feel that sensuality is overrated and certainly not very basic to your day-to-day happiness?

6. *Nurturance.* Do you like pampering? Does taking care of others, whether they be plants, pets, or people, make you happy? Or do you prefer to take care of yourself when you're tired or ill and to have others do likewise for themselves?

7. *Materialism.* Do you like to be chic and fashionable? Do you enjoy spending your leisure shopping

or window-shopping for designer clothes, jewelry, accessories, and other things? Or do you value simplicity and practicality and shun fashionable acquisitions?

8. *Extroversion.* Do you feel energized by being part of a group? Or do parties and meetings generally leave you drained? Do you draw energy from group situations and display your emotions easily (extrovert), or do you feel more comfortable alone or with just one other person (introvert)?

9. *Aestheticism.* Is the enjoyment of art, music, or nature's beauty important to you in everyday living? Do you like to spend your leisure time listening to music, visiting art shows, or seeing attractive scenery? Or do such experiences tend to bore you?

10. *Activity Level.* Are you constantly "on the go," charging from one activity to the next all day long? Or are you more of a "laid-back" person? The demands of work and career certainly affect our daily routines, so a better indicator of your real activity level is how you prefer to spend your weekends and vacations: Are you busily doing things, like hiking, jogging, or sight-seeing — or are you relaxing on your couch or at a poolside resort?

11. *Subjective Well-Being.* Are you usually optimistic in daily life? Is it your normal expectation that situations will turn out well for you? Or are you a worrier? Do you find yourself often regretting the past or becoming uneasy about the future?

12. *Intellectualism.* Are you an avid reader? Do you enjoy

discussing current events and future trends, as well as listening to news programs about such matters? Or do these activities generally make you yawn?

THE BIG 12 AS A TOTALITY

The evidence is clear: The more romantic partners match up on these twelve traits, the more joyful and long-lasting their bond will be. This perspective gives rise to four important issues. First, the Big 12 are as value neutral as the color of your eyes or hair. Whether you are high on Activity Level, Nurturance, Materialism, Libido, or any of the other eight traits makes no difference to us. Nor does it mean that you are better or more inherently successful. Rather, what's crucial is that you understand each of your intimacy characteristics so that you can find the best match for you: your personal soulmate.

Second, since perhaps 50 percent of your standing on these traits is inborn, there's nobody to blame, condemn, or overly praise. Indeed, mounting scientific evidence suggests that several Big 12 traits — such as Extroversion, Activity Level, and Libido — are probably much more than 50 percent genetically determined.

Third, if you initially find simplistic the concept that romantic intimacy depends on compatibility on twelve key personality traits, several helpful analogies exist. For example, physicists have long identified seven primary colors: red, orange, yellow, green, blue, indigo, and violet. While any child's crayon box reveals many dozen more — ranging from turquoise and maroon to silver and gold — all these other colors, while they may be beautiful, are considered secondary.

Likewise, scientists in the growing field of evolutionary

psychology have come to identify six human emotions as primary, that is, facially and most likely physiologically distinct and immediately recognizable across all cultures. Strikingly, even newborns react differently to facial expressions involving the primary emotions of fear, happiness, sadness, surprise, disgust, and anger. While people throughout history have certainly experienced a wider gamut of feelings (psychologist Robert Plutchik identifies more than 350) — such as amazement, cheerfulness, curiosity, hope, jealousy, and joy — these are increasingly viewed as derivative to the basic six emotions rooted in our biological makeup.

From our perspective, the insight that intimacy can finally be understood in terms of compatibility on twelve distinct personality traits makes bedrock sense. It frees everyone from unproductive finger-pointing and blame games. The issue for everyone becomes, "Do I match enough with this person on the Big 12 traits for love to be sustained?"

Fourth, we have found that it's necessary to understand people as totalities of these twelve traits in interplay, for each trait is independent of the rest. Fixating on just one trait tells us virtually nothing about the whole person. For example, just because Bill is extroverted, he's not necessarily high on Subjective Well-Being; rather, it simply means that he gets more energized in groups than in solitude. As lecturers and seminar trainers, we've often encountered extroverts like Bill who dominate groups and yet who are pessimistic, argumentative, and even hostile. It's certainly a mistake to assume that all extroverts are optimistic and cheerful.

Likewise, our Need for Companionship is a trait independent of Libido. Just because Todd has a strong yearning to share his feelings every day with a loved one doesn't necessarily mean that he desires frequent touching and sex. Conversely, there are plenty of people like Alison, who delights in foreplay and lovemaking with her partner but finds soul-baring conversations unnecessary and even tiresome. Or take the trait of Activity Level. Knowing that a person wakes up quickly and remains energetic all day long tells us nothing about his tolerance for Nurturance. There are men like Kevin, ranking high on both traits, who find it hard to sit still yet who enjoy pampering someone. And there are men like Marc, who are just as busy every moment but who stongly dislike nurturing.

Or let's look at Spontaneity. Knowing that Emily makes quick decisions and acts impulsively tells us nothing about her personality with regard to such traits as Idealism, Emotional Intensity, or Aestheticism. As someone who avoids planning and scheduling, Emily definitely may be idealistic, emotionally intense, and artistically oriented. Or she may just as likely be pragmatic, emotionally placid, and bored by art museums.

And Eric's high Extroversion tells us nothing about his Need for Companionship or his level of Materialism. Eric may be the life of the party, but he has little desire for soul-baring conversation or fashionable clothes. And Sonia's high Emotional Intensity does nothing to reveal — or predict — her Idealism or Intellectualism. Just because Sonia laughs and cries easily at movies doesn't mean that she embraces social causes like helping the homeless. Nor does it imply that she's not fascinated by current events.

WHAT DOESN'T MATTER

From time immemorial, men and women have sought intimacy in their relationships. Yet the psychological key to core compatibility has been lacking until now and has rendered this bond a hit-or-miss affair. The four artificial barriers of body type, gender, chronological age, and nationality have likewise constrained us. Because of the tremendous value of our new approach, each of these can now be overcome and understood as irrelevant and as stereotypes. Understanding the Big 12 traits and their vital significance in relationships gives us many benefits. Certainly, among the most crucial is a newfound clarity regarding what's relevant — and what's not — when it comes to sustaining lasting intimacy. Let us focus for a moment on these four barriers to intimacy.

Body Type

We've all heard stereotypes that associate diverse personality qualities with body type, such as joviality with girth and activity level with athletic build. However, we've found that the Big 12 traits are independent of physical characteristics, such as height and weight, eye color and other facial features, body type, and skin pigmentation. While physical "chemistry" is certainly important as a basis for intimacy, the components of lasting closeness are the Big 12, and these are wholly independent of such physical factors.

Gender

We've been long flooded with the stereotypes that all women are nurturing, that all men are highly active, that all women are emotionally intense, or all men are intellectual. These views are prevalent in many popular books, even best-selling ones.

Yet from our experience, such a perspective is both wrongheaded and erroneous when it comes to forging intimacy by finding compatibility based on the Big 12. It is clear, both from our forty years of combined counseling experience and from the thrust of personality research, that these stereotypes are not only irrelevant but also harmful. To put it simply, not all women are necessarily highly nurturing, spontaneous, or emotionally intense — and not all men are highly extroverted, libidinous, or intellectual. The fact that Danielle is a woman or that Alex is a man tells us nothing about their core personality traits. Thinking so is only a prescription for confusion. Understanding the Big 12 helps us finally to dispel these biases about gender.

In the old view, men were invariably high on Intellectualism and low on Nurturance, for instance, while women were seen as high on Nurturance and low on Intellectualism. Or all men as high on Libido and low on Need for Companionship, and all women as low on Libido and high on Need for Companionship. Or all women as high on Spontaneity and men as low on Spontaneity. These things have never been true, but owing to our acculturation, the core personality traits of both men and women have often been masked, repressed, or camouflaged. For example, women a few decades ago could enter only a small number of professions, such as education, nursing, or social work. Fortunately today, career choices are much wider; women can be lawyers, doctors, and architects, and men can be teachers and nurses. And increasingly, the same freedom to be oneself is expressed in romantic relationships.

AGE

As mentioned earlier, the core features of personality are typically manifested by early childhood, clearly apparent by adolescence, and relatively unchangeable throughout our entire adult lives. If three-year-old Jeremy delights in and thrives on music, you can be sure that he'll be avidly listening to it when he's nine, sixteen, twenty-seven, forty, and eighty-five. If eight-year-old Kaitlin enjoys reading books more than anything else, it's evident that she'll be consuming lots of literature in high school and later as an adult. And if Caroline is an emotional powerhouse in kindergarten, crying and laughing intensely in reaction to each day's events, she'll grow up to become a woman with similarly strong feelings about most things.

Of course, we all grow emotionally and spiritually as we get older. We all possess wisdom, and because it's so much a product of life experience, we usually become wiser with age. But our core personality traits involving intimacy — the Big 12 — do not change with advancing years. On this fact the growing body of psychological research is strikingly clear.

For this reason, chronological age has virtually no significance in determining personality compatibility. As long as you mesh on most of the Big 12 traits, whether you're twenty-five or sixty-five, is irrelevant. As long-standing prejudices and stereotypes about aging swiftly disappear today in the face of active, energetic men and women in their seventies, eighties, and even nineties, this point will seem clearer and clearer. If the two of you enjoy good physical "chemistry" and are highly compatible on the Big 12, even a big difference in chronological age is unimportant. Conversely, you and your prospective partner may be exactly the same age, but if you're not closely matched on these traits, your chronological parity means nothing. In this regard, we've no doubt that in coming years, chronological age will become less and less meaningful in influencing our choice of and commitment to our romantic partners.

NATIONALITY

Among the most salient findings in current psychological research is that core personality traits transcend cultural differences. That is to say, even if they are born and raised in countries as diverse as Japan or the United States, extroverts share certain key similarities — as do all those who are highly shy or anxious, empathic or enterprising. As we have already indicated, mounting evidence suggests that at least 50 percent of personality is innately determined rather than due to parenting or family values. To many of us, this viewpoint seems clear-cut.

But back in the 1930s and 1940s, cultural anthropologists had a very different viewpoint. It is important to note that they were consciously fighting against Nazism and racism, rooted in a brutal pseudo-biological viewpoint. Thinkers like Ruth Benedict, Margaret Mead, and Ralph Linton thus argued that basically nothing important about human personality is innate — rather, that "patterns of culture" (the title of Benedict's most famous book) determine everything about who we are as individuals. This seemingly enlightened view dominated social science for more than fifty years and was considered almost unchallengeable.

However, the increased sophistication of genetics and biological psychology — as well as the field of psychological testing — has steadily pointed in the opposite direction. Nationality or culture certainly affects our core personality, but it does not create it. Thus, Japanese and American extroverts share the same behavioral features of becoming energized in parties and group meetings and displaying their emotions easily. Similarly, two people who are low on Subjective Well-Being — who worry a lot about the future and feel personally vulnerable — make similar choices about life whether they live in England or Argentina.

What makes this finding important concerning love? To put it simply, our nationality and cultural background are much less relevant than was long believed when it comes to our basic personality. Just as differences in body type, gender, and chronological age are essentially irrelevant when it comes to compatibility for intimacy, so too is cultural variability. For example, twenty-four-year-old Sean is from Dublin, and thirty-year-old Leticia is from São Paulo, Brazil. They met in Rio de Janeiro while both were attending an international conference on music education. The two instantly felt a strong attraction to each other, but more important for achieving lasting intimacy, they shared high compatibility on many of the Big 12, including Aestheticism, Nurturance, Idealism, and Emotional Intensity. Although big cultural differences exist between Ireland and Brazil, Sean and Leticia share a promising Compatibility Profile (more about this in chapter 16). They plan to keep in touch, and their future together seems bright.

Let's put it another way. Anna is a thirty-one-year-old graphic artist from Italy who recently took a job in New York City with a major advertising agency. She is far more likely to forge lasting intimacy with a Californian who closely matches her Compatibility Profile than she is with a fellow Italian who differs significantly on the Big 12. Of course, language and culture can pose barriers to love. People must be able to communicate their feelings for one another and about life in general. But especially with the increasing ease, via the Internet, of meeting men and women around the globe, we're sure that nationality, like body type, gender, and chronological age, will fall as another artificial barrier to lasting intimacy.

What will decisively emerge will be the awareness that our uniqueness transcends these barriers. Choosing a romantic partner wisely will require awareness of our personality core — encompassing the Big 12 — in everyday life. The stakes are high, but it's definitely worth it! Before focusing on each of the Big 12 traits, let's have a little fun and see how they function in the everyday world.

CHAPTER THREE

THE BIG 12

IN ACTION

P sychology undoubtedly ranks as one of the most fascinating of all fields of knowledge. For what could be
more interesting than how we think, feel, and act toward each
other? And as a force for realizing the dream of a peaceful and
democratic humanity, it's certainly one of our most important
scientific endeavors. Yet, as a science that's about 120 years old,
psychology has often been accused by outsiders of "ivory tower"
speculation, that is, spinning notions about human behavior that
have very little relevance to everyday life.

Therefore, to help familiarize you with the "Big 12" in action
and to help you see that these personality traits are unmistakably
real — rather than irrelevant constructs — we've created this
thought-experiment. Just as the famed mathematician Albert
Einstein relied strongly on thought-experiments to highlight his

world-changing theories of space, time, and energy, we find that psychological thought-experiments can be highly effective in revealing vital aspects of human personality either overlooked or insufficiently recognized in our busy, day-to-day lives.

THE BIG 12 ON THE LOVE BOAT

So here we go. Imagine that you've been invited to a social gathering at a pleasant hotel conference room. Perhaps six months ago, just for fun, you entered a contest to win a trip. Last week you received notification in the mail from the contest company: Along with nineteen others from your area, you've won two free tickets for a nine-day Caribbean cruise, all expenses paid. The cruise line is well known, and there are no hidden charges. But for promotional and marketing purposes, the company has requested that all winners come to a publicity event where they'll be photographed, interviewed, and given their travel vouchers.

As you enter the conference room, you see a big buffet table filled with catered goodies. Festive balloons are everywhere, and there's up-beat recorded music in the background. A pair of marketing representatives welcomes you at the door. Checking your name on their clipboard roster, they smile, and one explains sheepishly, "We're running a little late. The video team will be here soon, and then we'll immediately start taping. So come in and enjoy yourself — there's a fantastic group of people here for you to meet!"

That's the background. Now, let's focus on the Big 12 and see how they manifest in this social situation. That is, what would you likely experience if everyone in the room — let's leave out the cruise line marketers — were identically high or low with regard to each of the Big 12 traits?

NEED FOR COMPANIONSHIP

If your nineteen co-winners ranked high on this trait, many would be accompanied by a friend to this event — and you'd see them milling restlessly in the hotel lobby. Expect nearly everyone to have a romantic partner or to be seeking a committed relationship. Conversations, therefore, would highlight romantic Caribbean "getaways" and "hide-outs" where couples could enjoy a marvelous intimacy without intrusion. Which cruise lines had the most amicable staff and provided the best ambience to form lasting friendships among fellow passengers would be prime topics too.

Beside the buffet table you'd hear people opening up about their personal lives: their families, friends, pets, past experiences, goals, and plans. By the time the videotaping was over, many among the group would have made a new acquaintance and exchanged phone numbers to get together soon. Most would exit the hotel still conversing deeply with one or two others.

However, if your co-winners all ranked low on Need for Companionship, the atmosphere would be decidedly cool. Virtually all would have arrived alone. The majority would be romantically unattached and content to stay that way. Depending on how many were extroverts, their conversations would either be boisterous or quiet — but definitely not soul baring. You'd hear nobody revealing personal matters about family or friends or sharing hopes and dreams. Among the group, there would be no desire to create friendships from this publicity event, and all would leave as alone as they had arrived.

IDEALISM

If the other nineteen winners were all high on Idealism, what could you expect? Many would be employed in such fields as counseling, ecology, education, nursing, or social work. Some might work for nonprofit agencies or own their own businesses, but few would likely to be corporate executives. Related to the upcoming Caribbean cruises, the winners' conversations might center on such topics as the region's environmental problems, poverty and illiteracy, and political corruption. Concerns about low wages and stressful working conditions in the cruise industry might also be addressed.

If the winners all ranked low on this trait, the talk would be very different. Certainly there would be minimal sympathetic interest in ecological problems, illiteracy, poverty, or social injustice in the Caribbean region. Instead of laments about the harsh working conditions faced by low-level cruise employees, there would be plenty of discussion about unreported island and shipboard crime, such as robberies, assaults, and rapes. There would surely be strong interest in how ship guests could best protect themselves from potential assaults and from rip-offs by local merchants and the cruise company itself, with its myriad "hidden" charges. Many among the twenty would enjoy recounting how they had outfoxed those who had tried to cheat them on past cruises and excursions — and especially which travel agencies in town had the worst reputations for "bait-and-switch" vacation package deals and other scams.

EMOTIONAL INTENSITY

If your co-winners all ranked high on this trait, the conference room would resound with strong feelings about nearly everything. When recounting their euphoria upon receiving notification of their award, the winners' joyful shrieks would be heard as far away as the hotel lobby. Jokes among pairs or small groups would provoke unrestrained belly laughs rather than polite titters.

Recollections of unpleasant tourist accommodations would be accompanied by unabashed anger or even tears. And in relating wonderful vacations from the past, faces would beam ecstatically. Almost everyone would be speaking animatedly.

But if your fellow contest winners were all low on Emotional Intensity, the atmosphere would be subdued. Nobody would be expressing much feeling about anything, not even the award notification. You'd certainly hear no raucous laughter, and no hot-tempered or tearful reminiscences. No one would be overtly happy or sad in sharing his or her stories, and no one would be listening empathically. The mood in the room would be as placid as a lake on a balmy summer day.

Spontaneity

If your co-winners all rated high on this trait, nearly everyone would arrive late — and a few probably not at all, having either forgotten to mark the event on their calendar or else lost the cruise ship's award-notification letter the night before. Most would be avid travelers, and they'd have lots of colorful stories about times they'd misplaced their luggage, missed their plane or ship, or been forced to take bizarre accommodations because of their last-minute travel decisions. Who had the most offbeat, unconventional, or exotic travel experience would be among the likely conversational topics, as well as which agencies were the most flexible in assisting with spur-of-the-moment touring adventures.

If your nineteen co-winners were all low on Spontaneity, everyone would have arrived early — or at least on time. Many would be carrying guidebooks, notepads, and laptops in order to amass as much information as possible about the itineraries. You'd hear lots of complaints that the cruise company had given only three weeks' advance notice about this event, and everyone would have already finalized their vacation plans for the rest of the year. Conversations would focus on which travel companies provide the best-organized tour packages of European countries (Asia or South America being too unpredictable) and which unfortunately fail to keep to their promised, hour-by-hour itineraries. At precisely the end of the videotaping, all would leave on time.

LIBIDO

In a room filled with nineteen of your fellow winners high on this trait, expect a lot of flirtatiousness and sexy clothing. Low necklines and tight-fitting attire would dominate. Whether originating among those single or married, the conversations would quickly shift to sex, sensual pleasure, and sexual adventures.

Steamy stories would be tossed around the room, and whether embellished or not, they'd evoke similar tales of hot nights spent with strangers encountered on other cruises and at island resorts. Both men and women in the room would exchange names of Caribbean clubs and bars with the best nightlife and pick-up opportunities. Certainly among singles, there would be a lot of touching, deep eye contact, and arrangements made to get together soon. An affair or two might well germinate from this gathering.

With a roomful of people low on Libido, expect the opposite. Conversations might arise about good places for family dining, interesting sporting and gaming events on various islands, and the best bargains for shopping. In fact, almost any topic could arise among the winners — with the exception of sex, sensuality, and sexual adventure. Indeed, many would talk eagerly about the best "family-oriented" resorts — and those lamentably catering to the "loose" and "wild" crowd. It's unlikely that any affairs would emerge from this gathering. And now, let's look at a very different trait.

NURTURANCE

If your fellow prizewinners were uniformly high on this trait, all would likely have dogs or cats at home. Except for those with severe allergies, some would undoubtedly own several pets. Finding a comforting "animal boarding home" during the cruise would therefore be a key conversational topic. And many of the questions directed at the ship's representatives would be about medical care for passengers: Is there a licensed physician aboard at all times? How well stocked is the infirmary? What kinds of arrangements are typically made for those with special dietary requirements, difficulty walking, or other health needs?

However, if your co-winners all ranked low on Nurturance, nobody would be particularly concerned about shipboard medical care. In their strongly held opinion, "People should take care of themselves." And because virtually none would be pet owners, their interest in the best boarding facilities for dogs and cats would be minimal or nonexistent. Indeed, this group would want explicit reassurance that no pets were allowed on board.

MATERIALISM

By their chic and fashionable appearance, your nineteen co-winners would make themselves known as high on Materialism. They'd all be wearing stylish clothing and have professional haircuts, and the women would be wearing makeup. You'd see lots of expensive jewelry, watches, and designer accessories. Many people would have arrived in fancy cars. Among this group, you'd hear lively discussions about luxury cabin suites and pricey décor — and of course, where to find the toniest boutiques, restaurants, pubs, and spas the Caribbean has to offer.

If your co-winners were all low on Materialism, you'd see everyone dressed in simple or outdated styles — and certainly no eye-catching jewelry. Handbags and briefcases would be plain. Conversations would include bargain-hunting triumphs and where to find brand-name clothing outlets and boutiques selling last year's styles at big discounts. How to save money on cruises would be a favorite topic too.

EXTROVERSION

If you were in a room for an hour with nineteen people who were all high on Extroversion, a lot of boisterous talking, laughing, and lively interaction would quickly occur. Within five minutes, everybody would casually introduce herself or himself to each of the other lucky winners. Before long, the gathering would get noticeably loud, adding to the excitement and free-flowing social energy. Small groups of threes or fives would rapidly form, with lots of joke telling, raucousness, and exchanges of business cards and home phone numbers. Everyone's facial expressions would be easy to read, and a few get-togethers and dates would probably be planned among some of the twenty. Nobody would be sitting or standing alone. The noise level would be so high by the time the video team arrived that the cruise line marketers would have to shout to make themselves heard. Amid more noisy laughter, jokes, and cross talk, the nineteen winners would almost reluctantly settle down to the business at hand.

Makes sense, right? Now imagine you've entered a room filled with nineteen people low on Extroversion. That is, they're all introverts. Almost nobody would be approaching anyone else to make an introduction. Each winner would be likely to sit down alone with food and beverage and to find the whole situation uncomfortable. To be forced to make small talk with a roomful of strangers might not rate as their worst nightmare, but it certainly would be on their list of events definitely to avoid. The noise level in the room would be low, even after ten or fifteen minutes. There would be no bellowing laughter or mutual backslapping, and it's likely that several winners would have left the room to call their office, look for a newspaper, or use some other excuse to act on their unease. Most would be silently immersing themselves in the brochures and hoping the whole thing would soon be over. Networking and lively socializing among the twenty would be minimal, and no subgroups would be likely to emerge. Facial expressions would be hard to read, and when the marketers announced that the video team had arrived, everyone would be relieved that this uncomfortable experience was finally over. Got you convinced?

AESTHETICISM

If your nineteen co-winners were all high on this trait, many would be amateur musicians, artists, or photographers, and at least a few would earn their living this way. Among the group, you'd spot portable CD players and sketch pads and hear plenty of talk about Caribbean music and art — and where to find the most gorgeous vistas for taking photographs. Conversations would also focus on interesting art galleries, museums, concert halls, and music clubs around the islands. Undoubtedly there'd also be lively discussion on the variety and quality of the cruise ship's musical entertainment.

But if your co-winners were all low on Aestheticism, you would hear none of this "arty" talk. Instead, experienced island-hoppers would reminisce and exchange advice on the best places to shop, eat, or drink. And if the topic of previous visits to Caribbean art galleries, museums, and music venues came up at all, you'd only hear complaints like, "What a waste of time! I was bored to tears!"

ACTIVITY LEVEL

If your fellow contest winners were uniformly high on this trait, they'd surely look fit and trim for their age. Most would never have been on a cruise before, having avoided such seemingly slothful vacations. Their questions for the cruise representatives, therefore, would focus on the kinds of shipboard activities available: Is there an indoor track? Does the largest pool accommodate lap swimming? What kinds of exercise equipment does the fitness center offer? And how late does the entertainment go every night? Conversations would center on opportunities for aquatic sports like snorkeling and island hiking trails.

Conversely, if your group consisted of all those low on Activity Level, few individuals would appear athletic. Generally, you'd hear questions geared to cabin comfort — that is, how to create a personal nest aboard: a "home-away-from home" as quickly and easily as possible. Nobody would be terribly concerned about the fitness center's latest equipment, the largest swimming pool's exact dimensions, or opportunities for marathon jogging. Much more relevant for these folk would be the cabin's design and bedding, the availability of extra blankets and pillows, and the variety and serving hours of drinks, snacks, and full meals. The comfortableness of deck chairs for daylong relaxing and sleeping would likely be another conversational topic.

SUBJECTIVE WELL-BEING

If your nineteen co-winners all ranked high on this trait, you'd enjoy a delightful afternoon. Everyone would be pleasant, good-natured, and optimistic about the upcoming cruise. You'd hear lots of compliments being exchanged. Smiles would be everywhere. The room would glow with reminiscences about past vacations, and even major mishaps would be described with humor. The "silver lining in the clouds" would be dominant.

If your fellow winners were all low on Subjective Well-Being, worry and pessimism would reign supreme. You'd hear so many reports of miserable experiences aboard ship — or involving vacations in general — that canceling your award and taking the small cash substitute right now might begin to seem the only sensible decision. Reminiscences about wretched past cruises and foreign trips would not only lack the proverbial silver lining, they would be downright depressing. Conversations would be laced with sarcasm, bitterness, and anger. It's likely that arguments and even trades of insults would arise — and depending on the degree of emotional intensity in the room, these could become rather heated. But look on the positive side: You'd feel great when you left this group behind at the hotel!

INTELLECTUALISM

If the conference room were filled with those high on this trait, you'd see a lot of people carrying newspapers, magazines, or books. And while some of these books would undoubtedly be the latest international spy thriller or horror novel, plenty of reading material would feature current politics, biographies, and future trends. The conversations would glitter with advanced vocabulary, frequent references to writers and thinkers, and of course, to important events happening now in the world.

If your group were uniformly low on this trait, anticipate the opposite. Few would carry anything other than a local newspaper as reading matter, and even fewer a nonfiction work or literary novel. While the conversations might cover many subjects, you can be sure that new ideas, history, or emerging social trends would not be among them.

Now that we've envisioned these traits in action, let's move on to looking at each of them in detail.

PART TWO

THE
BIG 12

CHAPTER FOUR

NEED FOR COMPANIONSHIP

"Are you lonesome tonight?" crooned Elvis Presley in his famous song by the same title in 1960. A lot has changed since that era, except certainly for basic human desires, hopes, and longings. It's clear to us — then as now — that some men and women have a strong yearning for close bonding in everyday life — for sharing their innermost thoughts and feelings with a loved one — whereas others definitely prefer keeping people at an emotional distance.

It's clear from the many songs that Elvis wrote and sang lamenting loneliness and separation between lovers that the King of Rock and Roll almost certainly ranked high on the important personality trait we call Need for Companionship. And it's likely, with regard to such songs, that his greatest fans were those who shared this feature of the Big 12.

For a long time, therapists mistakenly believed that everyone was more or less identical in their need for others. Their unproven — and naive — assumption was that individuals who lack deep friendships, or who seek firm boundaries in their intimate relationships such as marriage, are somehow repressed neurotically, that if only they were given the right therapeutic treatment, they would lose their "fear of intimacy" and start to bare their souls. Paradoxically, many therapists also promulgated the view that those who get lonely easily and have a strong desire to share their daily joys, disappointments, and hopes with a true intimate are likewise neurotic and in need of overcoming such "overdependency" by learning to accept — and even embrace — emotional solitude.

Today, both viewpoints are as antiquated as electric typewriter ribbons. While the evidence is still far from conclusive, it's increasingly clear that dating back to our earliest days of childhood, we differ significantly from one another in how much closeness we desire in our bonds, initially with immediate family members, and later with relatives, peers, neighbors, teachers, mentors, co-workers, and others in our social environment. How much distance we prefer emotionally certainly is in itself neither healthy nor unhealthy, but it does have tremendous impact on romantic intimacy. And while the way we are raised by our parents certainly affects our personal Need for Companionship, that it's a trait significantly innate now seems incontrovertible.

EARLY SIGNS

While virtually all infants learn to bond with a trusted loved one — typically but certainly not always their biological mother — they differ strikingly in how close they prefer that bonding to be. Those high on Need for Companionship tolerate maternal separation much less easily than others; they dislike being left alone in their crib even for short periods. Later, in preschool years, they often find it emotionally painful to leave home for nursery school or kindergarten. Not long ago, psychologists dubbed this phenomenon *separation anxiety* and blamed parents for making their offspring seemingly "overly dependent." Accordingly, professional advice focused on how to minimize such dependency.

Fortunately today, it's increasingly understood that all children — and teens — differ temperamentally in their need for personal closeness; this trait is also most likely greatly innate rather than due to parenting. Long before high school graduation, some youngsters already enjoy deep friendships destined to last decades — if not a lifetime — whereas others are content with casual relations and will never form "bosom" friends. Generally, girls in the United States are more likely than boys to verbalize their companionship needs; but from our professional experience, the trait can be strong or weak in either gender.

BEYOND STEREOTYPES

People with a strong need for companionship are often stereotyped as neurotic, clingy, or overly dependent. This mischaracterization is typically applied to women who desire emotional closeness in a relationship. The reality is far different, for the degree of distance you prefer to keep toward others has nothing to do with mental health or illness. However, your standing on this trait certainly has many implications. Not only are you better off paired with someone well matched, but it's also important concerning your work and career.

SELF-QUIZ ON
NEED FOR COMPANIONSHIP

Please read each question carefully and mark the answer that best fits you. There are no right or wrong answers, and you need not be an "expert" to take this quiz. Just describe yourself honestly and state your opinions as accurately as possible. Be sure to answer each item. If you make a mistake or change your mind, erase your answer completely. Then mark the number that corresponds to your correct answer.

- Mark a 1 next to the statement if it's *definitely false* or if you *strongly disagree.*
- Mark a 2 next to the statement if it's *mostly false* or if you *disagree.*
- Mark a 3 next to the statement if it's *about equally true or false,* if you cannot decide, or if you are neutral on the statement.
- Mark a 4 next to the statement if it's *mostly true* or if you *agree.*
- Mark a 5 next to the statement if it's *definitely true* or if you *strongly agree.*

_____ 1. I must admit I'm a hard person to get to know.

_____ 2. I have a strong need for companionship.

_____ 3. I dislike people who want to know what I'm feeling.

_____ 4. I can't imagine how people can live alone for many years and be happy.

_____ 5. Having close friends matters a lot to me.

_____ 6. I usually know what people are feeling.

_____ 7. I like going off on vacations by myself.

_____ 8. I am a very private person.

_____ 9. I enjoy going to the theater or movies by myself.

_____ 10. Having someone to share my hopes and dreams is vital to me.

_____ 11. Being a loyal friend is very important to me.

_____ 12. I like keeping others at an emotional distance.

_____ 13. I need friends who really listen to me.

_____ 14. I like going to events with someone close.

_____ 15. I don't have many close friends, and that's fine with me.

_____ 16. I enjoy being with someone even if we don't talk much.

_____ 17. People who need close friends to be happy are weak.

_____ 18. It's important for me to share my feelings about the events of my day.

_____ 19. I find it hard to make friends easily.

_____ 20. I am annoyed by people who want to tell me how they feel about things.

_____ 21. I don't have a strong need to share my feelings.

_____ 22. I enjoy having a drink with a close friend.

DETERMINING YOUR SCORE

- Add up the numbers you wrote by statements 2, 4, 5, 6, 10, 11, 13, 14, 16, 18, and 22.

  Total for part A_____

- Now subtract the numbers by statements 1, 3, 7, 8, 9, 12, 15, 17, 19, 20, and 21.

  Total for part B_____

Your score on Need for Companionship is A minus B:_____.

INTERPRETING YOUR SCORE

Scores on this self-test of Need for Companionship can range from −44 to +44.

If you have scored 22 or more, then you are *high* on Need for Companionship. It's important to your daily well-being for you to share your hopes, disappointments, and dreams with someone emotionally close to you. Concepts like "respecting personal boundaries" and "allowing for personal space" are hard for you to fathom, much less put into real practice. Cultivating and sustaining friendships mean a lot to you. It's easy for you to get hurt or feel rejected by those who don't share your strength on this trait — or for you to dismiss them as shallow. You crave soulful depth with others. The more you can achieve it with someone you care about, the greater your sense of fulfillment.

If you scored 21 or less, then you are *low* on the Need for Companionship. Of course, you may like many people and have good friends, but you typically keep such relationships light and casual. Only in rare circumstances — and then only briefly — do you get involved in intense, soul-baring conversations. For such behavior seems not only immature and self-indulgent to you but also intrusive. In your perspective, personal space and relationship boundaries are serious matters. As the poet Robert Frost so aptly put it, "Good fences make good neighbors."[1]

NEED FOR COMPANIONSHIP: THE FOUR SCENARIOS

YOU BOTH SCORE HIGH

It's time to celebrate, for you've created a bond in which you can both satisfy your strong soul-baring needs. In a world filled with

---

1   Robert Frost, "Mending Wall," in *North of Boston* (New York: Henry Holt, 1915).

men and women who emphasize emotional boundaries and live by Frost's motto, you each have a partner interested in deeply sharing hopes, dreams, longings, disappointments, frustrations, pleasures, and joys. And you enjoy this not just on rare occasions involving major life events like births or weddings but also on an ongoing daily basis, when nothing "special" seems to be happening.

Neither of you has to feel embarrassed or apologetic any longer about becoming lonely easily or thriving best in the company of a trusted friend. You're each well suited now, able to reveal your private self to one who appreciates, welcomes, and indeed *desires* such intimate communication as vital to love.

You'll definitely spend a lot of time and energy responding to one another's thoughts and feelings. Questions like, "What did you dream about last night?" "What are you daydreaming about now?" And "What was the best thing that happened to you today?" keep both of you animated and happy. It's not surprising, therefore, that even temporary separations between you — business trips or visits to far-off relatives — will be jointly hard to bear, and even painful. For each of you craves deep companionship in the depths of your souls. From the smallest events of each day to major life events, you'll always have plenty to talk about together.

Your greatest challenge? To embrace the reality that no matter how wonderfully close you each feel to your partner, we all need boundaries. Space is necessary for growth as individuals. If

---

BELIEVE IT OR NOT...

- If your partner is high on Need for Companionship, he quickly gets lonely.
- If your partner is low on Need for Companionship, she doesn't want to have soul-baring conversations.

you can keep that phrase as your watchword, your days and nights will indeed be golden.

You Both Score Low

You two undoubtedly agree with Robert Frost's viewpoint! For you both know and respect the importance of boundaries in relationships. That people need both privacy and room to grow as individuals in this busy world is basic to your outlook. To smother your partner emotionally in order to feel appreciated or loved is totally foreign to your makeup.

Your bond will include lots of personal space. You definitely won't feel the need to be right next to each other very often. Even while home together, you'll prefer to be

> ## IF YOU FIND YOURSELF THINKING...
> - *Doesn't my partner ever open up?*
>   You're involved with someone low on Need for Companionship.
> - *Doesn't my partner ever just make casual small talk?*
>   You're involved with someone high on Need for Companionship.

doing something individually — and to like it that way. Let other couples constantly dwell on their thoughts and daydreams, disappointments, hopes, and daily reactions to life's little events.

But certainly not you. Not only would such a pattern seem unnecessary — and almost silly and obsessive — it would make you both feel downright uncomfortable. Why subject yourself to daily interrogations? You each believe that keeping a healthy distance among people allows peace and harmony to flower.

Neither of you needs close friends to feel happy or fulfilled in daily living. And getting heavily involved emotionally with siblings — not to mention with uncles, aunts, and cousins —

GREAT EXPECTATIONS

- If your partner is high on Need for Companionship, expect to hear about her dreams and daydreams.
- If your partner is low on Need for Companionship, don't expect him to bare his soul very often.

has never been your personality style. Thus, when making plans for yourself as a pair, you'll be able to focus primarily on just you and your partner. In your view, everything is much simpler this way.

Occasional separation from your love partner feels quite bearable to you. If he or she must travel alone for business or extended family matters, you don't feel rejected or crushed. Nor does the proverbial roof collapse over you. Needing little emotional stroking to feel valued, you can go about your everyday routine with a minimal sense of emptiness.

Your greatest challenge? While you have each discovered that you are your own best friend, the reality is that, as poet John Donne asserted, "No man is an island entire of itself." This point is especially important for those sharing your preference for personal boundaries. If you deliberately share your deeper feelings each day — especially when the impulse arises — your island will indeed be a paradise in full bloom.

YOU SCORE HIGH, BUT YOUR PARTNER SCORES LOW

Be forewarned: you're going to feel lonely often in this relationship. There's no simpler way to say it, and there's really no point in offering pleasant euphemisms like "Just accept the fact that your partner needs more personal space in daily life than you do." Not only is such advice patronizing, it's also absurdly ineffective.

For the bottom line emotionally for you won't change an iota, no matter what soothing pseudo-therapeutic words are offered — either now or later. If you hear this kind of advice from a well-meaning friend or even a counseling professional, reject it immediately. Or even better, flee from it. Basic to your personality is the wonderful need for someone really close, someone deeply interested in your innermost longings, hopes, disappointments, joys, and dreams. And just as important, you need someone seeking the same delicious closeness. But with your partner, know that's not going to happen. With events large and small, in everyday living, you're going to feel distressingly isolated — and often down-right ignored and rejected. Frequently when you have an interesting thought or experience to share, he or she won't be responsive and indeed may become annoyed if you persist in pressing the conversation. You may feel your unique, innermost world cherished by a like-minded friend or by solitary journaling if you're so inclined, but definitely not by this bond.

> ### WHAT YOUR PARTNER LIKES TO HEAR
>
> - If your partner is high on Need for Companionship, ask, "What did you dream last night?"

Conversely, you'll often want to know what your partner has been thinking or experiencing during the day, and "nothing special" will be the terse reply. You may feel ignored to the point that you start imagining the day when he or she will cast off the need to keep people at an emotional distance like an old cloak — and will finally want to sustain deeply beautiful intimacy. But in your heart, you know that's purely an enticing fantasy.

Be aware too: From your partner's perspective, you're intrusive and disrespecting of his or her right to reasonable privacy.

Sure, your intent is admirable, but you reflexively come off as pushy and even a boundary-violator. And so? The harder you metaphorically struggle in trying to forge soul-baring closeness, the more your partner will pull away. It's called dancing alone.

YOU SCORE LOW, BUT YOUR PARTNER SCORES HIGH

"He travels fastest who travels alone," declared the great British novelist Rudyard Kipling. These are admirable and accurate sentiments in your view — but definitely not in your partner's. You'd better get used to it now: You'll be battling constantly about where to draw the line — and even about, believe it or not, whether there should be a line — when it comes to setting boundaries between you two emotionally, physically, and domestically. Be amply forewarned: Your partner would prefer virtually no distance at all.

For you, true intimacy always involves — and indeed requires — a deep respect for each other's personal space. In your strongly held outlook, it's obvious that everything — people just as much as flowers — needs room to grow and that having a clear privacy zone is essential for making love last. You have no desire to push and probe at the feelings of those you know, to penetrate their private world of disappointments, hopes, and longings, or to escort them into your innermost domain.

WHAT RUFFLES YOUR PARTNER'S FEATHERS

- If your partner is high on Need for Companionship, he gets ruffled when feeling alone.
- If your partner is low on Need for Companionship, she gets ruffled when expected to reveal innermost thoughts.

Truthfully, none of that excites or even interests you very much. You'd much rather talk about current events around the world, fashion, movies, music, or travel than to hear people's dreams, yearnings, and goals. What's wrong with this personality style? Unfortunately, for your partner it's reflective of coldness and indifference and signals that you really don't give a hoot about what's important in his or her own daily life. Your sincere, even gentle, efforts to give personal privacy will be interpreted as little more than selfishness and detachment.

Conversely, expect to be subjected to a barrage of invasive questions from your well-meaning partner. Daily — or even more often — you'll be asked how you're feeling, what you're thinking and planning, and whether today is proving the same as or different from yesterday. Your inclination will definitely be to keep such distracting and annoying conversations to a minimum, but this strategy is sure to make your partner feel hurt and rejected. The higher you politely try to build the privacy barrier, the harder your partner will try to tear it down.

If only your partner could emulate Henry David Thoreau, who asserted, "I never found the companion that was so companionable as solitude." Then you might finally enjoy space, peace, and harmony in your relationship. A delightful dream to be sure, but it's never going to come true.

> ### EXPRESSING AFFECTION: GIFT-GIVING AND COMPLIMENTS
>
> When your partner is high on Need for Companionship:
> - Give her his-and-her matching outfits.
> - Compliment his ability to be so open.

CHAPTER FIVE

IDEALISM

Would you rather think of yourself as basically idealistic or as basically pragmatic? Make a choice, right now. If you overheard someone emphatically describe you as a "do-gooder," would you feel complimented or put down — and why? When writer Finley Peter Dunne wryly urged, "Trust everyone but cut the cards," was he being overly cynical about human nature, or absolutely realistic?

The Big 12 trait known as Idealism is among the most important affecting our daily lifestyle. It encompasses our central image not only of humankind — that is, whether we regard individuals as essentially honest and trustworthy — but also of human existence itself, spanning the domains of religion, spirituality, mysticism, ethics, and morality.

Our position on this trait colors virtually everything we do in our day-to-day lives — including how we treat our parents, siblings, children, friends, neighbors, and co-workers; it embodies much more than simply our voting preferences, political attitudes, or even the extent of our charitable donations and volunteerism. Not surprisingly, therefore, many psychologists now believe that with the possible exception of Libido, conflict between partners concerning Idealism is the most destructive of all to intimacy. This insight is hardly new. We didn't need the advent of the scientific study of temperament to tell us that regardless of their wealth or status in life, some people believe in doing good deeds, helping others less fortunate, and devoting their lives to making a better world. Other men and women from exactly the same religious or social background display only sneers for those living by this credo.

While probably less biologically based than our Activity Level or Libido, our level of Idealism similarly seems to transcend parental and cultural influences. As psychologist Abraham Maslow argued in his famous "hierarchy of human needs" approach to motivation, virtually every society in history has generated truly selfless and saintlike men and women as well as those who have totally rejected this outlook.

Can two people who are in love and otherwise admirably matched conflict strongly on this personality trait? Yes. It happens all the time. Is one likely to convince, or change the other to the opposite view? Almost never.

EARLY SIGNS

More than any of the other Big 12 traits, Idealism seems influenced by parental upbringing. Although there's increasing evidence that even this trait probably has a genetic basis —

researchers are calling it our "religious gene" — it seems clear that our perspective on human nature and world betterment include values that, as young children, we learn from adults. Because toddlers and preschoolers — not to mention babies — lack the language skills to be measured on this trait, most research has focused on youngsters of kindergarten age and older.

The findings are consistent throughout the world. When it comes to compassionate ("moral") reasoning and concern for justice, children show striking differences. Some boys and girls place a high value on acting unselfishly, generously, and even courageously when faced with moral dilemmas involving people presented in stories or videos. Others, who are just as intelligent, express the attitude, "That's his problem, not mine," and display little interest in deciding the best course to follow ethically or heroically. Certainly, by high school, some teens are actively involved in ecological and social causes, taking on the world's problems, such as pollution, homelessness, and injustice, as a personal challenge. Others show no interest or are even cynical about such seemingly impractical matters. While it's possible for individuals to change their standing with regard to Idealism after adolescence, the likelihood is small.

BEYOND STEREOTYPES

It's often assumed that people high on Idealism are also quite caring in their daily routine, but that's not always true. Indeed, it's not unusual to meet people who sincerely espouse sympathy for a wide variety of social and ecological causes but who have no desire to pamper or to be emotionally supportive of family members, co-workers, or others they know personally. It's not really a contradiction, for, as we'll see, Nurturance and Idealism are really different traits.

SELF-QUIZ ON IDEALISM

Please read each question carefully and mark the one answer that best fits you. There are no right or wrong answers, and you need not be an "expert" to take this quiz. Describe yourself honestly and state your opinions as accurately as possible. Be sure to answer each item. If you make a mistake or change your mind, erase your answer completely. Then mark the number that corresponds to your correct answer.

- Mark a 1 next to the statement if it's *definitely false* or if you *strongly disagree.*
- Mark a 2 next to the statement if it's *mostly false* or if you *disagree.*
- Mark a 3 next to the statement if it's *about equally true or false,* if you cannot decide, or if you are neutral on the statement.
- Mark a 4 next to the statement if it's *mostly true* or if you *agree.*
- Mark a 5 next to the statement if it's *definitely true* or if you *strongly agree.*

_____ 1. "Nice guys finish last" is a saying with a lot of truth to it.

_____ 2. To climb the ladder of success, you have to step on people.

_____ 3. I believe in a Higher Power that guides us all.

_____ 4. People are basically dishonest.

_____ 5. We're all put here in this world to do good.

_____ 6. I believe that each of us should make the world a better place.

_____ 7. I never trust someone I don't know well.

_____ 8. People who follow the Golden Rule are only asking to be taken advantage of by others.

_____ 9. In my view, miracles happen.

_____ 10. As I go through life, it's important for me to help others.

_____ 11. Each of us has a special mission in life.

_____ 12. "Honesty is the best policy" is definitely my viewpoint.

_____ 13. As a wise saying has it, "It's a dog-eat-dog world."

_____ 14. I trust most people.

_____ 15. "Looking out for number one — me!" is my philosophy.

_____ 16. People who give money to charities are suckers.

_____ 17. People will help you if you give them the chance.

_____ 18. Doing volunteer work is a waste of time.

_____ 19. People who believe in a Higher Power are just kidding themselves.

_____ 20. I feel that all men and women are brothers and sisters.

_____ 21. I would certainly keep a bag of money I found on the street if I knew nobody would learn of it.

_____ 22. "The world is a wonderful place" is my philosophy.

DETERMINING YOUR SCORE

- Add the numbers you wrote by these statements: 3, 5, 6, 9, 10, 11, 12, 14, 17, 20, and 22.

    Total for part A_____

- Now subtract the numbers by these statements: 1, 2, 4, 7, 8, 13, 15, 16, 18, 19, and 21.

    Total for part B_____

Your score on Idealism is A minus B:_____.

INTERPRETING YOUR SCORE

Scores on this self-test of Idealism can range from -44 to +44.

If you scored 22 or more, then you are *high* on Idealism. You believe that people are basically honest, good, and trustworthy. You feel that most people will prove their true worth if just given the chance. It's your view that human existence has a higher purpose than "dog-eat-dog" or the "rat race" and that each of us has a role to play in helping to make this a better world. Supporting social causes is thus important to you. Perhaps you're also interested in spirituality and mysticism, involving angels, reincarnation, synchronicity, psychic experiences, and divination tools like astrology, Kabbalah, and tarot. To achieve true intimacy, you'll definitely need a partner who shares this outlook.

If you scored 21 or less, then you are *low* on Idealism. In your perspective, people cannot be counted as trustworthy and honest until so proven. "Show me" is your motto. And while you may wish you had some of the faith in human goodness touted by altruists, you certainly would not follow in their path devoting time and energy to social causes, volunteerism, and charitable activities. In a world you see filled with suckers, losers, and victims, you want to be among the triumphant. For you an intimate partner would need to be similarly tough-minded.

BELIEVE IT OR NOT...

- If your partner is high on Idealism, he regards most people as trustworthy and honest.
- If your partner is low on Idealism, she regards most people as selfish and out for "number one."

IDEALISM: THE FOUR SCENARIOS

YOU BOTH SCORE HIGH

You two are a genuinely altruistic couple, trying to make the world a better place for us all. While many men and women are mainly seeking to just get through each day with a minimum of hassles — or worse, to outfox and triumph over others — you both really want to use your time on earth to make it a kinder, gentler, and more harmonious world.

We'll say it forthrightly: this isn't an attitude you are faking, as in the famous description of the industrial titan Andrew Carnegie: to "win friends and influence people." No, it is a perspective on human nature, ethics, and doing good deeds that is as basic to you as your eye color and blood type. Be glad that you each have a partner who shares this humanitarian outlook, for you will have many fulfilling experiences together.

> **IF YOU FIND YOURSELF THINKING...**
>
> - *Doesn't my partner ever stop wanting to change the world?*
>   You're involved with someone high on Idealism.
> - *Doesn't my partner ever want to make the world a better place?*
>   You're involved with someone low on Idealism.

Certainly, the two of you may choose to volunteer actively at various periods in your life, devoting time and money to ecological, economic, or political causes. You may decide to open your door as well as your checkbook — and not merely your hearts — in the philanthropic domain. But more basically, you will have similar feelings, reactions, and goals when it comes to confronting injustice and reducing unnecessary suffering in our communities and the wider world. As a pair you'll enjoy accepting people at face value, seeking their best qualities, and overlooking their flaws. You may also get pleasure from jointly exploring spiritual practices like meditation, martial arts, and various types of mysticism.

GREAT EXPECTATIONS

- If your partner is high on Idealism, expect lots of sympathy for social causes.
- If your partner is low on Idealism, don't expect much concern for the disadvantaged.

Your greatest challenge? Accepting that practicalities, including paying the rent or mortgage, grocery and medical bills, and taxes are really part of your life together — and won't disappear simply by wishing it so. If you can balance your altruistic and lofty impulses with some pragmatic sensibility, you can indeed have it all.

You Both Score Low

When circus impresario P. T. Barnum reportedly proclaimed more than a century ago, "There's a sucker born every minute," he certainly wasn't thinking of you two. For like Barnum, who became internationally famous and rich by capitalizing on people's gullibility, you too see the world as filled with lambs and wolves. While the biblical prophet Isaiah predicted a day when these species would lie down together, you both know it hasn't happened yet in two thousand years — and you're not holding your breath.

In daily living, you both enjoy being careful and protective about your possessions, savings, and achievements. Knowing well that ever more skillful scams and rip-offs abound in our high-tech society — just look at the burgeoning white-collar crime of identity theft — you like warning each other, and being warned about, the ranks of charlatans and con artists out for fresh victims. Sharing your cynicism about phony charities and volunteer agencies is another source of mutual satisfaction.

Credit card companies with exorbitant fees masked by incomprehensible disclaimers, telephone solicitors offering get-rich-quick investments, dishonest accountants, electronic mer-chandise stores with bait-and-switch tactics, slick vacation package and time-sharing promoters, unscrupulous home land-scapers, swimming pool installers and aluminum-siding sales-people — and of course, blatantly crooked automobile repair shops: The list truly seems endless and is probably limited only by your own imagination.

In this vein, you'll find lots to talk about. And most likely, you'll make friends with individuals and other couples

> ### WHAT YOUR PARTNER LIKES TO HEAR
>
> • If he or she is high on Ideal-ism, say, "Tell me about a good deed you did for someone today."

who are similarly vigilant against the world's never-ending deceit. Further, you and your partner will take pride in distancing your-self from those who naively believe that the Golden Rule really works in life, that good deeds are aptly rewarded, and especially that "we are all brothers and sisters." Hasn't anyone who espouses this viewpoint seen how contentious siblings can become in fighting over Mom's or Dad's property? In the classic words of Marvel Comics impresario Stan Lee, " 'Nuff said."

Your greatest challenge? To be open to new ventures and experiences that may initially seem dubious but that may lead you onto new paths of happiness together.

You Score High, but Your Partner Scores Low

Believing as you do in the Golden Rule and possibly as well in miracles, get ready for a lot of stressful soul-searching regarding the higher purpose of your relationship. For you're paired with someone who sees human events, large and small, through a radically different lens than you do. Your first impulse in judging people and situations is always to see them in the most favorable light. "Until proven otherwise, everyone should be trusted" is your philosophy. You want to make the world a better place. But your partner sees your outlook as impractical and unrealistic, and even as a prescription for personal ruin. It's no wonder that therapists view discord on this trait as among the most insurmountable in love relationships.

You'll often find yourself shocked, bewildered, and hurt by your partner's seeming callous and cold-blooded concern with the "bottom line" in your life together. Your kindly interest in social and ecological causes, your staunch support for charitable organizations and volunteerism of all kinds will likely be greeted with pseudo-paternalistic advice like "you should look out for number one" — or outright sarcasm about your seeming naiveté. If you actually plan to write checks or donate your time to helping others in need, expect heated arguments with little resolution.

WHAT RUFFLES YOUR PARTNER'S FEATHERS

- If your partner is high on Idealism, he gets ruffled by seeing injustice and inequality.
- If your partner is low on Idealism, she gets ruffled when people sympathize with the poor, homeless, or disadvantaged.

Count on clashes too on many other aspects of everyday living. These may well encompass such diverse matters as spending priorities, investment plans and goals; relations with friends, relatives, and neighbors; choice of where to live, community involvement; child-rearing values; and what meaningful work or career to pursue. If you're interested in spirituality and the paranormal — such as going for astrological or psychic readings — your partner is likely to view these matters as flaky and a foolish waste of money. How do you think all this will make you feel?

> ### EXPRESSING AFFECTION: GIFT-GIVING AND COMPLIMENTS
>
> If your partner is high on Idealism:
> - Give a donation in his name to a charity or social cause.
> - Compliment her social compassion and spirituality.

You Score Low, but Your Partner Scores High

We know you don't like life to be sugarcoated, so here it is straight from the shoulder: You're going to be constantly disagreeing with someone whose basic values and philosophy seem hopelessly naive to you. Daily, over matters large and small — from paying utility bills to federal taxes, from recycling garbage to discussing the latest news events and planning major vacations — you will have conflict. Why? Because you see the world through a much harsher lens than your partner does, and no matter how much you value this relationship, you'll feel continually frustrated by what you consider his or her gullibility, superstition, and downright spaceyness.

More than occasionally, you're likely to wish with all your heart that your partner would just grow up and finally realize that people are untrustworthy, dishonest, and selfish. Or that some Santa Claus in the sky really isn't taking tabs on "who's been bad and who's been good" — and dispensing rewards accordingly. Or that organizations calling themselves charities and seeking money and volunteers are actually run by those interested in making a fast buck, like everyone else.

But know this: Your partner isn't going to change and one day become realistic and sensible. Instead, for as long as you can imagine, you're going to hear about his or her sympathy for a multitude of social causes, many of which will strike you as patently ridiculous. When you point out headlines related to massive fraud and indictments, it will be to little or no avail. If your partner also has a mystical bent, you're going to be exposed to his or her "foolish" openness to astrologers, psychics, mental massagers, and alternative healers of every stripe and persuasion — all promising wonderful health and contentment in return for the right fee. However patiently you point out the reality of the situation, you'll find yourself accused of being shallow, uncaring, and mercenary.

On a mundane level, you'll find yourself having to protect your partner innumerable times from would-be scams and rip-offs — whether coming in the mail, over the phone, or even at your doorstep. Don't expect to be thanked for your vigorous concern. Rather, you're likely to be criticized for being narrow and heartless — even paranoid — in your lack of faith in people's innate goodwill and kindness. Your own best impulses will be consistently rejected.

CHAPTER SIX

EMOTIONAL

INTENSITY

Do you consider yourself an emotional person? If a potential friend candidly described you that way to your face, would you be flattered or disturbed? Compared to most people you know, are you stronger in the intensity and range of your feelings, milder, or somewhere in between?

Whereas for centuries astute observers of the human condition have noted that people vary remarkably in this dimension — it's been the theme of many great novels — only recently have psychologists come to understand that this difference is already apparent on our first day of postnatal existence — and continues strikingly unchanged ever after. As a vital component of the Big 12, Emotional Intensity clearly plays a major role in love relationships, yet has oddly been all but ignored professionally.

The vast realm of our feelings is clearly experienced differently by people across cultures. For example, it's long been a truism that those from Mediterranean backgrounds — such as Italians, Greeks, Spanish, and Portuguese — are typically more emotionally open and demonstrative than Northern Europeans like the Swiss and German, and the British. Similarly, South Americans and Caribbean Islanders are regarded as more emotionally expressive than their North American counterparts. The field of cross-cultural psychology is still in its infancy, but such seeming stereotypes have recently been found to contain more than a kernel of truth. Nevertheless, in every culture and country, some people are definitely more emotionally intense than others — and interestingly, they may be drawn to the same kinds of work and professions. For instance, whether growing up in Chicago, Paris, or Hong Kong, teachers of young children are likely to thrive on vivid emotionality, whereas accountants are likely to prefer rationalistic activities each day.

In terms of gender, in the Western world, historically women have been depicted as being more dominated by their feelings than men, for example; they're commonly thought of as making major decisions based on moods rather than hard facts. But there's virtually no scientific evidence to back this up. Indeed, anyone who has ever grown up in a family indisputably knows that many men are volatile emotionally, and lots of women conversely express a placid inner world.

What's clear, though, is that it is more acceptable for women to show strong emotions — such as tears of sadness or shock — in work or other public settings than it is for men. And perhaps more important, the two genders often have different ways of expressing the same emotion, whether it be love or gratitude, jealousy or envy, sympathy or fear, affection or generosity. For example, men rarely cry when feeling sad. But when it comes to a relationship involving two particular people, the intensity of their emotions is always what ultimately matters.

EARLY SIGNS

Emotional intensity is among our most basic personality traits. Infants and even newborns vary significantly on this vital quality. Obstetricians know this well, vividly describing some babies' "lusty cry" after their birth. In the first few months of infancy, the emotions of pleasure, distress, surprise, disgust, joy, anger, and somewhat later, fear and sadness, are specifically identifiable in all. But as every parent discovers, some babies express these vigorously, while others are quite placid.

At age five, emotionally intense children cry and laugh with great feeling; for example, they become distraught when a family pet is sick or hurt and ecstatic when opening birthday gifts. As a preteen, he or she already reacts strongly to movies and favorite TV shows, and when feeling upset, may spend hours moping. By high school, many can't watch horror movies but feel deep pleasure at happy events like religious confirmations, "sweet sixteen" parties, graduations, and prom nights. Whatever the feeling, the pitch is intense.

BEYOND STEREOTYPES

It's common to confuse Emotional Intensity with warmth, friendliness, and likability. Yet this trait reflects how strong a person's feelings typically are in daily life, not how positive or pleasant they are. Indeed, nearly everyone has met people prone to acute anger, sadness, fear, or jealousy but rarely those disposed to vibrant cheerfulness, gratitude, admiration, or joy. Regardless of the specific feeling, those high on Emotional Intensity will express them all forcefully — never meekly or mildly. A feeling is a feeling, and for those emotionally intense, the river runs deep, no matter its name.

SELF-QUIZ ON
EMOTIONAL INTENSITY

Please read each question carefully and mark the one answer that best fits you. There are no right or wrong answers, and you need not be an "expert" to take this quiz. Describe yourself honestly and state your opinions as accurately as possible. Be sure to answer each item. If you make a mistake or change your mind, erase your answer completely. Then mark the number that corresponds to your correct answer.

- Mark a 1 next to the statement if it's *definitely false* or if you *strongly disagree.*
- Mark a 2 next to the statement if it's *mostly false* or if you *disagree.*
- Mark a 3 next to the statement if it's *about equally true or false,* if you cannot decide, or if you are *neutral* on the statement.
- Mark a 4 next to the statement if it's *mostly true* or if you *agree.*
- Mark a 5 next to the statement if it's *definitely true* or if you *strongly agree.*

_____ 1. I must admit that I'm a rather emotional person.

_____ 2. I cry easily at sad or romantic movies.

_____ 3. Sentimental songs seem silly to me.

_____ 4. Whatever my mood, I usually feel it intensely.

_____ 5. I usually have strong feelings about people I meet.

_____ 6. I like people who approach life in a logical rather than emotional way.

_____ 7. I usually try to control rather than express my feelings.

_____ 8. Sometimes when reading something sad in the newspaper, I get tears in my eyes.

_____ 9. Many people seem like "cold fish" to me.

_____ 10. When making an important decision, I pay more attention to the facts than to my feelings.

_____ 11. I would be too embarrassed to cry in front of others.

_____ 12. I often laugh aloud in the theater at funny movies.

_____ 13. When making an important decision, I listen most to my feelings.

_____ 14. My feelings are on the mild side.

_____ 15. I get upset easily.

_____ 16. I'm glad to admit I'm not an emotional person.

_____ 17. I almost never cry at a movie.

_____ 18. Most people seem overly emotional to me.

_____ 19. I love with real passion.

_____ 20. I like to keep my feelings well hidden from others.

_____ 21. People who laugh aloud at movie theaters annoy me.

_____ 22. I sometimes have tears when listening to sentimental music.

DETERMINING YOUR SCORE

- Add the numbers you wrote by these statements: 1, 2, 4, 5, 8, 9, 12, 13, 15, 19, and 22.

    Total for part A_____

- Now subtract the numbers by these statements: 3, 6, 7, 10, 11, 14, 16, 17, 18, 20, and 21.

    Total for part B_____

    Your score on Emotional Intensity is A minus B:_____.

INTERPRETING YOUR SCORE

Scores on this self-test of Emotional Intensity can range from −44 to +44.

If you scored 22 or more, then you are *high* on Emotional Intensity. Whatever you're feeling as you go through the day, it's likely to be strong. Your emotions flow like a river, and sometimes the current surges so strongly that you feel swept along. When you love, you're passionate. When you're happy, you're buoyant. And that's great. But alas, when you're angry, you're furious, and when you're sad, you can grow depressed. For you, the world often seems filled with "cold fish" who lack your emotional energy. So intimacy is best sustained with a warmly reactive rather than a placid partner.

If you scored 21 or less, then you are *low* on Emotional Intensity. You deal with life in a calm, even-tempered manner. Very little ruffles your feathers, and you like it that way. Rarely do you feel yourself lurching up and down on an emotional roller-coaster; for you, the ride is smooth. As you move through the everyday hustle and bustle, you often wonder why the world seems filled with so many hotheads and loose cannons. In your experience, intimacy is emotionally low-key — certainly a rewarding journey, but with neither soaring peaks nor plunging valleys.

EMOTIONAL INTENSITY: THE FOUR SCENARIOS

YOU BOTH SCORE HIGH

Life for you two is a powerhouse of feelings, charged continually by your inner batteries. Even your dreams are likely to be more vivid than those of others, either glorious or alarming.

Psychologists have come to identify more than 350 different emotions in human affairs, and don't be surprised if together you get to know — and experience — them all.

You may as well congratulate yourself on the fullness of your happy times ahead, for they'll be marvelously happy indeed. What for many couples are small or even trivial pleasures — like a walk in the park, a leisurely drive, or an entertaining movie — often positively captivate you.

Unlike those who require blockbuster moments in life to feel animated and exhilarated, countless events during a normal week can propel you jointly into an uplifting frame of mind. It's a wonderful gift to experience delights so easily.

But you should also know that depending on the level of Subjective Well-Being you share, little disappointments, hurts, or frustrations can easily become magnified. When it comes to minor understandings between you, you may each tend to make mountains out of proverbial — and ephemeral — molehills. Reality checks are therefore particularly useful. Don't be afraid to use your head, and not just your heart, for guidance. It can also be helpful to ask a friend, perhaps someone low on Emotional Intensity, for advice if you're feeling downcast. Your greatest challenge on your life's rolling sea? Accepting that highs and lows are intertwined and that just as light cannot exist without darkness, your capacity to feel intensely as a team encompasses many moods. Keep focusing on the positive, let memories of your best times together be your beacon, and joy will be yours.

You Both Score Low

"Nothing to excess" advised the Greek statesman and poet Solon more than two millennia ago, and you two would absolutely agree. In your shared view, the world is filled with hotheads, loose cannons, and in-your-face emotional displays of every type. As all the articles about road rage, air rage, and now desk rage keep saying, the problem continues to worsen. "Letting it all hang out" emotionally is becoming our new international sport — so much so that simple courtesy and civility seem to be rapidly disappearing.

You're thus glad to experience — and react — to life's events with a persistently calm demeanor. You're both even-tempered and placid, and perhaps have even been accused of being complacent. But so what? In many ways, complacency is just another word for contentment, those with your trait might justifiably argue — and isn't that the goal for all of us? Indeed, growing medical evidence suggests that frequent catharsis — that is, uncontrolled venting of anger or sadness — not only isn't good for our well-being but it also seems to increase the risk of heart disease by placing our body-mind system on continually stressful "high alert."

> ### IF YOU FIND YOURSELF THINKING...
>
> - *Doesn't my partner ever laugh or cry at a movie?*
>   You're involved with someone low on Emotional Intensity.
> - *Does my partner have to get so emotional about everything?*
>   You're involved with someone high on Emotional Intensity.

As a couple, your moments of emotional heat together will be minimal — and this will suit you just fine. Keeping things light and low-key in all matters comes naturally to both of you. As you may already sense, the heady fountain of passion and excitement will cascade somewhere else, as will the engulfing torrents of disappointment, bitterness, and sorrow. Your emotional pond will be beautifully smooth.

> **GREAT EXPECTATIONS**
> - If your partner is high on Emotional Intensity, expect strong feelings in most situations.
> - If your partner is low on Emotional Intensity, expect reactions based on reason most of the time.

Visitors to your home will immediately notice your soft-spoken way of life together. Certainly you will have dreams and hopes, desires and longings — but these will be consistently mild and easily contained if necessary. Individually and as a pair, you'll almost never feel like victims of your feelings but rather like their confident guide and master.

Your greatest challenge on your placid emotional sea? To know as a couple that lightning often strikes without warning and that storm clouds sometimes burst. If you can accept life's inevitable emotional storms when they arise, greater harmony is assuredly within your grasp.

YOU SCORE HIGH, BUT YOUR PARTNER SCORES LOW

Whether you are joyfully sitting on top of the world or sadly moping down in the dumps, don't be surprised if you feel that you're going through life paired most of the time with a cold fish. For whether you're watching an endearing romantic movie, listening to sentimental music, reading a gripping news article, or simply recapping your day's triumphs and disappointments, your emotions play a vital, starring role. You can't be any different, and there's no reason for you to be.

But to your partner, facts are always more important and even more interesting than feelings. No matter how hard you try, no matter what strategies you adopt, you won't be able to raise his or her Emotional Intensity to your level. The surface — and the depths too — are placid. If you think this discrepancy is a prescription for discord and hurt, you're absolutely right.

WHAT YOUR PARTNER LIKES TO HEAR

• If he or she is high on Emotional Intensity, say, "Do you want to hear something hilarious?"

When you have happy, wonderful news to relate — a job promotion, a new business deal, a child's accomplishment — your partner will react in a way that seems lukewarm or even frigid. When you're upset, sad, or downright depressed and are looking to be cheered up, you'll likewise feel let down. But know that your partner is not trying to hurt, trivialize, or marginalize you. He or she simply doesn't get excited by very much, for good or for bad, in experiencing life. And don't even begin to imagine that beneath your partner's complacent demeanor lies someone destined one day to emerge crying and laughing with beautiful intensity like you. It won't happen, and to expect it to is only a self-delusion. The more you press to elicit a big reaction, the greater your partner's back-off will be.

Also be aware that from your partner's perspective, your

seemingly endless emotionality is stressful and wearing. Virtually any strong feeling you display, even laughing giddily or crying at a lively movie, will seem immature and an embarrassment. Each of you longs for an emotional state the other cannot provide.

YOU SCORE LOW, BUT YOUR PARTNER SCORES HIGH

Count on it: Because of your partner's personality, you're going to become acquainted with lots of different emotions — more intense and varied than you have probably ever imagined. Of course, you've met demonstrative people in the past. But this is different, it's your relationship, and virtually every day now you're going to be presented with vivid emotions as never before. Rare indeed will be the movie that fails to provoke tears or belly laughs in your partner, regardless of how others are reacting.

Your basic approach to life emphasizes that problems are challenges to be solved log-

> ### WHAT RUFFLES YOUR PARTNER'S FEATHERS
>
> - If your partner is high on Emotional Intensity, he gets ruffled when people are reserved.
> - If your partner is low on Emotional Intensity, she gets ruffled when people show strong feelings.

ically, and that feelings, however intriguing to some people, are really only secondary to facts. Like the renowned Mr. Spock in the popular *Star Trek* TV series, you regard human emotions as fascinating, baffling, or disturbing — but never as a reliable guide for acting in this world. To do so would be the height of foolishness. But your partner has the opposite view.

With this combination, expect lots of discord in your reactions to friends, relatives, neighbors, work and career, and countless other elements of daily life. You'll feel that you're paired with a walking firecracker — someone who has strong feelings about nearly everything — from the salad bar's diversity at the local Italian restaurant to the personality of all your siblings — and everything in between.

> ### EXPRESSING AFFECTION: GIFT-GIVING AND COMPLIMENTS
>
> When your partner is high on Emotional Intensity:
> - Give him a heady perfume or cologne.
> - Compliment her passion and facility with emotions.

You'll thus find yourself asking over and over again, "Can you please lower your voice?" or "Can you please calm down?" or "Just take a deep breath and then let's talk, okay?" But far from proving reassuring, your gently worded comments will only irritate and even enflame your partner, for in his or her eyes you're detached emotionally from what really matters — and generally don't care about the relationship at all. And do keep in mind that behind your partner's vivid emotionality there's no placid, low-key person waiting quietly to step forth. Whether you're watching the news, discussing the day's events, or planning your next vacation, get set to be faced with continually strong feelings.

CHAPTER SEVEN

SPONTANEITY

D o you like to take chances? Do you get bored easily and consider yourself a risk taker? Do you regard the old sayings "nothing ventured, nothing gained" and "fortune sides with one who dares" as shrewd advice? Or is this outlook really an invitation for foolish mistakes and failure? After all, the celebrated Chinese philosopher Confucius declared millennia ago that, "The cautious seldom err." Did he have it right?

The personality trait of Spontaneity has been the subject of seemingly endless and contradictory maxims through the ages. We've all heard "trust your gut," "go with the flow," and "above all, seek a life of adventure" as well as "look before you leap," "fools rush in where angels fear to tread," and "above all, seek a well-ordered life." Ultimately all these wonderful adages cancel themselves out — leaving each of us to choose an appropriate course for ourselves, based on who we are. And probably that's exactly how it should be, for as psychologists, we seriously doubt whether even the most beautiful proverb can really alter someone's behavior and core personality.

This observation appears especially true when it comes to Spontaneity. In the business world, it's been increasingly identified as a key personality trait of entrepreneurs and has been recently linked genetically to a behavioral preference for new stimuli, traceable back to early childhood and even infancy. Unlikely to be the result mainly of how we were raised, our tendency to act impulsively versus methodically in everyday life is deeply ingrained.

Indeed, organizational researchers find that a discrepancy between co-workers on this particular trait is the most likely of all to cause conflict. This makes eminent sense: If you're orderly and a planner, it would definitely be frustrating for you to share an office with someone who is diametrically the opposite. By all evidence, this pattern seems to be true for love compatibility as well.

EARLY SIGNS

From an early age, children differ widely on how much they enjoy — and seek — new stimuli in their environments. Indeed, there's evidence that newborns differ greatly when it comes to this basic personality trait. Some babies chortle with pleasure and obvious delight when presented with new shapes or objects in their crib, whereas others immediately become fretful, irate, or fearful. As parents can readily affirm, some preschool children become bored easily and demand new experiences often. Others, however, are content to enjoy the same toys over and over again or to watch the same video almost endlessly. Psychologists now believe that the desire for novelty — that is, Spontaneity — strongly predicts many behaviors in later life, including entre-preneurialism, as mentioned above. By high school age, those high on Spontaneity are identifiable to peers and family as impulsive, as poor planners, and as risk-takers. They often do things on a dare, and they dress and act unconventionally. Although their intelligence may be high, their schoolwork and belongings are usually untidy and disorganized. In contrast, teens low on Spontaneity prefer routine and predictability. They enjoy attending clubs with regularly scheduled times for activi-ties, and their belongings and school materials are kept neat and orderly.

BEYOND STEREOTYPES

If you think that people high on Spontaneity are necessarily carefree and outgoing, think again. They are just as likely to be worriers and shy around others. This trait solely concerns impul-sivity versus planning and decision-making and preference for new experience versus routine. And, regardless of TV and movie images, there's no proof that men are inherently lower on Spon-taneity than women.

SELF-QUIZ ON SPONTANEITY

Please read each question carefully and mark the one answer that best fits you. There are no right or wrong answers, and you need not be an "expert" to take this quiz. Describe yourself honestly and state your opinions as accurately as possible. Be sure to answer each item. If you make a mistake or change your mind, erase your answer completely. Then mark the number that corresponds to your correct answer.

- Mark a 1 next to the statement if it's *definitely false* or if you *strongly disagree.*
- Mark a 2 next to the statement if it's *mostly false* or if you *disagree.*
- Mark a 3 next to the statement if it's *about equally true or false,* if you cannot decide, or if you are *neutral* on the statement.
- Mark a 4 next to the statement if it's *mostly true* or if you *agree.*
- Mark a 5 next to the statement if it's *definitely true* or if you *strongly agree.*

_____ 1. I rarely plan anything more than a few weeks in advance.

_____ 2. Making changes is hard for me.

_____ 3. "Be careful in all that you do" isn't a useful approach to success.

_____ 4. I avoid going to unfamiliar restaurants.

_____ 5. I don't mind entering a new situation without careful planning.

_____ 6. I trust my intuition more than getting facts.

_____ 7. I have routines, and I stay with them.

_____ 8. I like to do something new every day.

_____ 9. On vacation, I like to plan each day's activities as carefully as possible.

_____ 10. People who don't plan much get on my nerves.

_____ 11. I like to seek out new parks and places to visit.

_____ 12. I must admit that I find it hard to stick to routine.

_____ 13. I must admit that I often act on impulse.

_____ 14. People who like to plan things carefully often get on my nerves.

_____ 15. I select my words carefully.

_____ 16. I am a planner.

_____ 17. I pick and choose slowly when shopping.

_____ 18. On my vacations, I like to have lots of unplanned time.

_____ 19. I use forethought in all I do.

_____ 20. I like to stay with the tried-and-true.

_____ 21. I can't understand why some people need to plan everything in their lives.

_____ 22. I like to eat the same foods every day.

DETERMINING YOUR SCORE

- Add the numbers you wrote by these statements: 1, 3, 5, 6, 8, 11, 12, 13, 14, 18, and 21.

    Total for part A_____

- Now subtract the numbers by these statements: 2, 4, 7, 9, 10, 15, 16, 17, 19, 20, and 22.

    Total for part B_____

Your score on Spontaneity is A minus B:_____.

INTERPRETING YOUR SCORE

Scores on this self-test of Spontaneity can range from −44 to +44.

If you scored 22 or more, then you are *high* on Spontaneity. Doing something new each day is appealing. You like to make decisions quickly, even on the spur of the moment, trusting your intuition that "everything will work out fine." You're adventurous, even impulsive — typically deciding on plans without much consultation, prior thought, or regard to their practicality. To those who differ with you strongly on this trait, you can truly seem like a "loose cannon" in your sudden plans and actions. For you intimacy is best achieved with someone who shares your excitement for new experiences.

If you scored 21 or less, then you are *low* on Spontaneity. You thrive on daily routine and structure and embrace the familiar. "A place for everything and everything in its place" is your motto. You take pride in being a planner, paying close attention to details so that everything is orderly and coherent. You make decisions methodically rather than intuitively. You also dislike surprises and taking chances and seek to minimize these experiences. For you, intimacy involves enjoying what life has to offer in a stable and orderly way.

SPONTANEITY: THE FOUR SCENARIOS

YOU BOTH SCORE HIGH

You two will be doing lots of things on the spur of the moment. Because you both prize flexibility and keeping all options open, together you'll enjoy a sense of freedom about life's events, big and small. On a typical day, weekend, or vacation, your watch-words will be, "Go with the flow. Let it happen naturally."

As a couple, you'll feel happiest and most exuberant when your time is unplanned. Suddenly deciding on a stroll or drive, a night out — or even a two-week foreign trip — feels com-fortable and raises no hackles for either of you. Indeed, it's who you both are. What others view as sheer impulsiveness — would *impetuous* be too strong a word? — is for your type exactly what gives day-to-day living its spice and excitement.

Only reluctantly, sometimes only when absolutely necessary, will you jointly enter the unpleasant, bothersome — and, let's admit it — intimidating realm of details and schedules. On one side of the coin, you'll certainly find yourself benefiting from your laid-back perspective. By not planning anything very much, you allow both serendipity ("happy accident") and syn-chronicity ("meaningful coin-cidence") frequently to lead you into delightful experi-ences and connections. The feeling that any given day is wonderfully unpredictable may even exhilarate you spiri-tually. But on the flip side, expect stresses and hassles —

> **BELIEVE IT OR NOT...**
>
> - If your partner is high on Spontaneity, she tends to act on impulse.
> - If your partner is low on Spon-taneity, he seeks to plan virtu-ally everything.

and possible arguments — because the two of you waited until the last minute before choosing where to go and what to do.

Your greatest challenge? Accepting and respecting that the "three Rs" of rules, regulations, and routines (relax, we're not including regimentation!) are not only unavoidable in your life together, but they are even necessary and desirable. If you can adopt this attitude while cherishing your attraction for the new, the sky's the limit.

YOU BOTH SCORE LOW

One thing is for sure: You two will be a well-organized pair, enjoying days and nights that are carefully planned and that harbor a minimum of surprises. "A place for everything and everything in its place" is your recipe for successful and contented living. You agree with Ben Franklin, who advised more than two centuries ago, "Look before, or you'll find yourself behind."

That's right. Let others take financial and personal risks, gambling their possessions and health with leaps into the unknown. Not the two of you, who regard most problems — and even failures in life — as due to hastiness and lack of foresight. Rather, "moderation in all things" and "slow and steady wins the race" are your mutual credos. Undoubtedly you've each felt this way since your childhood.

You prefer dining at familiar restaurants, vacationing at familiar resorts, and enjoying an orderly procession of days and seasons. When it comes to shopping for anything from groceries to appliances, you agree that preparing lists beforehand saves lots of time and energy. If you are making larger purchases for items such as furniture, automobiles, or houses,

---

IF YOU FIND YOURSELF THINKING...

- *Doesn't my partner ever do anything on impulse?*
  You're involved with someone low on Spontaneity.
- *Doesn't my partner ever plan ahead?*
  You're involved with someone high on Spontaneity.

---

you will both want to do ample research. Both of you relish planning trips and vacations in careful detail — and consequently, will find using the Internet — not just as a research tool but as a means to rely on the "tried-and-true" — a pleasurable activity.

It's likely that you'll choose individuals and couples as friends who share your disdain for impulsiveness, risk-taking, and sudden whims, especially those who seek new experiences "just for the hell of it." In your view, that's never the way to find happiness; it's only a prescription for calamity.

As a couple, your greatest challenge is to listen some-times to that little voice in your head calling out, "Just do it!" If you can heed this beckoning, it will lead you onto joyful paths of intimacy that you never dreamed existed.

> **GREAT EXPECTATIONS**
>
> - If your partner is high on Spontaneity, expect lots of spur-of-the-moment decisions.
> - If your partner is low on Spontaneity, expect lots of careful planning and consideration.

You Score High, but Your Partner Scores Low

Organizational experts have found that discord on this trait causes more conflict among co-workers than any other, and to paraphrase actress Mae West, "It ain't too good for couples either." Your natural tendency is to do things impulsively, live fully in the moment, and let the future take care of itself. It's important for you to have as much flextime as possible to enjoy life and savor all its unexpected delights. For what could be more pleasurable than the sense of freedom from routine and rules?

Alas, your partner has a very different perspective, and it's almost impossible to balance both views well. In direct contradiction to yours, his or her approach to daily living is careful, orderly, and methodical. As a result, you'll find yourselves arguing over countless matters, big and small, with little satisfying resolution. You don't like planning ahead; it makes you feel confined. But your partner equally dislikes scheduling things at the last minute. You enjoy making spur-of-the-moment decisions about where to dine, what new movie to see, and who to join for fun this upcoming weekend. To your partner, that's a sure prescription for needless stress and chaos.

> **WHAT YOUR PARTNER LIKES TO HEAR**
>
> • If he or she is high on Spontaneity, ask, "Where can we go that's new and different?"

You'll constantly be feeling defensive about your freewheeling outlook, as well as relentlessly regimented by your partner. You'll feel tied to a "control freak," while your partner will feel paired with a "loose cannon."

Note well: As time passes, this discrepancy will become more noticeable and pervasive, not less. Why? Because shared lives inevitably become more intertwined and complicated. No matter how hard you try, you won't succeed in turning your partner into someone adventurous and risk-taking. And no matter how intensive his or her efforts may be, you won't become a cautious planner who thrives on predictability. As you probably know by now, this disharmony is particularly blatant when it comes to vacations. While your ideal is a block of days or even weeks that are marvelously unplanned, that's precisely your partner's vision of misery in the making.

You Score Low, but Your Partner Scores High

Gird yourself for a relationship with someone who's nearly always disorganized, imprudent, and careless about plans. Not only is your partner not going to change, but, as you'll soon discover, he or she will be perfectly content to stay that way. What to you seems an obviously self-defeating and even self-destructive way to live, filled with last-minute frenzies, missed appointments, and needless tension, gives your partner a gratifying sense of freedom.

The more you try to structure your time together sensibly, the greater will be his or her rebelliousness and rejection of all your diligent efforts. You'll often feel like an exasperated or even angry parent lecturing a wayward child when it comes to your partner's seemingly scatter-brained approach to daily life.

While doing things on impulse may be acceptable — even endearing — in an out-

> **WHAT RUFFLES YOUR PARTNER'S FEATHERS**
>
> - If your partner is high on Spontaneity, he gets ruffled when faced with long-range planning and details.
> - If your partner is low on Spontaneity, she gets ruffled when faced with impulsivity .

going five-year-old, it's certainly not when displayed repeatedly by an adult. At times, you may feel particularly distressed by irresponsible changes in plans for dinner, shopping, socializing, or entertainment that he or she makes — suddenly altering everything on whim, seemingly "just for the hell of it." If this isn't the definition of selfishness, then what is?

Expect vacations to be a major source of conflict. You prefer to plan each day carefully, not to mention thoroughly researching the accommodations and surroundings. The painstaking hours you spend on the Internet will yield a wonderful payoff, but you'll receive little gratitude for your activity — and you may even be criticized as "rigid," a "killjoy," and a "control freak."

What you see is what you get. Deep down inside your impulsive partner no careful planner lurks, biding time before he or she becomes well organized like you. The gushing, spur-of-the-moment decision-maker — who sees every day as an opportunity for adventure — is here to stay.

EXPRESSING AFFECTION: GIFT-GIVING AND COMPLIMENTS

When your partner is high on Spontaneity:

- Make a reservation for a new restaurant or resort.
- Compliment her sense of adventure and risk-taking.

CHAPTER EIGHT

LIBIDO

Do you think of yourself as having a strong libido? For you, is romantic intimacy filled with sensual desire and delight, or does all that seem the fluff of silly movies and novels? Do you frequently long for unrestrained embracing? And does the biblical Song of Songs, celebrating the raptures of physical love, affirm your sense of glorious spirituality, or basically leave you cold?

For thousands of years, poets and thinkers have written about our libidinous impulses. While psychologists today debate its influence across the overarching range of human life — even Sigmund Freud famously admitted that sexual symbolism can be taken to extremes when he said, "Sometimes a cigar is just a cigar" — there's no doubt that in love relationships, libido has huge impact. And while past puberty nearly everyone experiences erotic desires at least occasionally, it's become increasingly clear scientifically how strikingly people differ on this Big 12 trait.

The evidence is now indisputable that both men and women show marked variability in the domain of eroticism. Medical laboratories in many countries report distinctly similar findings. Whereas some people become physiologically aroused frequently and quickly — and respond strongly to a wide variety of stimuli, ranging from photographs, artwork, movies, and stories to self-generated fantasies — other individuals from identical educational or religious backgrounds become excited only rarely and slowly and respond mildly, if at all, to explicit sexual materials. It likewise appears definite that physiological response, personality, and sexual attitudes are all intertwined. That is, people who become aroused often and easily are usually those who regard sex more favorably — and enthusiastically — than those whose erotic threshold is contrastingly high. As the saying goes, "What you see is what you feel."

So where does this variability originate? More and more, the signs point to innate hormonal differences displayed by both men and women rather than to parental or community influence. While much remains to be discovered about broader aspects of libido, apart from sexual arousal — such as desire for caressing, stroking, and sensual touching in general — the contours of this research already seem clear. Much about sex may "be in the head" as the popular adage notes, but it definitely begins in the body.

EARLY SIGNS

While it's often been noted that boy babies show erections and girls like to rub their lower bodies against anything they come up against, there's no evidence that such behavior actually involves the sexual impulse. Rather, psychologists find that childhood libido can be inferred by observing such behaviors as curiosity and attachment. While people in the United States and other industrialized countries are now having sex at younger and younger ages, there are definite markers for when most people start becoming sexual beings: For girls, it's at menstruation, when they become aware they can have babies, and for boys, it's when they begin to have nocturnal emissions and fantasies about girls their own age or older.

Usually by preteen years, and definitely by early adolescence, those high on Libido show strong interest in the opposite sex. Girls may wear makeup and dress provocatively in bare midriffs, push-up bras, high heels, and tight-fitting clothing to attract attention — or flirt overtly with older male teens. Boys are likely to seek out pornography in magazines, X-rated videos, or via the Internet. Certainly, masturbation is likely to be frequent. By the way, there's no indication that such early interest in sexuality is a product of parental permissiveness or encouragement; often parents are genuinely shocked to discover that their young teen is already sexually active. Generally, adolescents high on Libido are more likely than others to date at an early age, to "go steady," and to engage in premarital sexual activity.

BEYOND STEREOTYPES

Many people blithely use the phrase "sexually active" as synonymous with having libido. But men and women with a strong sensual drive aren't necessarily high on Activity Level. Indeed, they may prefer lots of lounging and nesting and shun traveling. Some evidence exists for women, however, that those who work out regularly experience more libidinous desire and enjoyment. There's certainly no indication that physically active recreation, like jogging, hiking, and cycling is a substitute, secret or otherwise, for eroticism.

SELF-QUIZ ON LIBIDO

Please read each question carefully and mark the one answer that best fits you. There are no right or wrong answers, and you need not be an "expert" to take this quiz. Describe yourself honestly and state your opinions as accurately as possible. Be sure to answer each item. If you make a mistake or change your mind, erase your answer completely. Then mark the number that corresponds to your correct answer.

- Mark a 1 next to the statement if it's *definitely false* or if you *strongly disagree.*
- Mark a 2 next to the statement if it's *mostly false* or if you *disagree.*
- Mark a 3 next to the statement if it's *about equally true or false,* if you cannot decide, or if you are *neutral* on the statement.
- Mark a 4 next to the statement if it's *mostly true* or if you *agree.*
- Mark a 5 next to the statement if it's *definitely true* or if you *strongly agree.*

_____ 1. I think sex is overrated.

_____ 2. I can't imagine myself enjoying a gallery of erotic art.

_____ 3. Sexual attraction isn't vital to me in choosing a romantic partner.

_____ 4. I dislike it when people tell jokes about sex.

_____ 5. People who look at pornography on the Internet have a big problem.

_____ 6. I find myself sexually attracted to a lot of people.

_____ 7. I like sex to be leisurely, like a form of art.

_____ 8. I have very sexy dreams.

_____ 9. I need a lot of hugging and physical affection to feel romantically happy.

_____ 10. Children should be taught that masturbation is wrong and should be avoided.

_____ 11. I try to be creative in sexual positions.

_____ 12. I enjoy many forms of caressing during sex.

_____ 13. I enjoy being nude with my partner and enjoy looking at ourselves.

_____ 14. I like to dress in a sexy way.

_____ 15. Many people have too much sex drive for their own good.

_____ 16. My sexuality is an important part of who I am.

_____ 17. I don't like being touched a lot during sex.

_____ 18. There's something wrong with people who have sexual fantasies.

_____ 19. I dislike people who want a lot of hugging and touching.

_____ 20. Sex certainly isn't important in my life.

_____ 21. I enjoy watching pornographic movies.

_____ 22. I masturbate and think it's normal and healthy.

DETERMINING YOUR SCORE

- Add the numbers you wrote by these statements: 6, 7, 8, 9, 11, 12, 13, 14, 16, 21, and 22.

    Total for part A_____

- Now subtract the numbers by these statements 1, 2, 3, 4, 5, 10, 15, 17, 18, 19, and 20.

    Total for part B_____

Your score on Libido is A minus B:_____.

INTERPRETING YOUR SCORE

Scores on this self-test of libido can range from −44 to +44.

If you scored 22 or more, then you are *high* on Libido. You celebrate your sexuality and that of your partner. Sensuality is important to you; you experience your body as a source of erotic pleasure. It's satisfying for you to touch your partner often and to be touched often as well. You view sexuality as something natural and positive. Its expression in pictures, movies, books and magazines, conversation and humor — and, of course, intimacy — are enjoyable to you.

If you scored 21 or less, then you are *low* on Libido. Sexuality is not a priority for you. Sensuality is not your way of relating to the world. The eroticism of your body and that of others is not vital to your well-being. Touching and being touched often are not pleasurable, and sexuality has little value in your life. Its expression in pictures, movies, conversation, and humor does not allure you. And when it comes to sustaining intimacy, you use means other than sexuality.

BELIEVE IT OR NOT...

- If your partner is high on Libido, he desires lots of touching and lovemaking.
- If your partner is low on Libido, she is satisfied with a quick kiss now and then.

LIBIDO: THE FOUR SCENARIOS

YOU BOTH SCORE HIGH

You two will definitely enjoy frequent touching, embracing, and sensual play. Whether carousing in bed or on the living room couch — or in more exotic locations at home or away — you won't feel forced to make time for such frolicsome activity. Rather, doing so will come as naturally as arranging your schedules or eating or sleeping.

You both will want to caress and be caressed on a daily basis, or close to it. While you may both certainly desire more — or less — sensuality together at various times, you'll instinctively understand its importance to each other's well-being and happiness.

For both of you, feeling loved has a strong physical component. No matter how beautiful, tender, or passionate, words alone won't satisfy your heart. And yet, compared to many couples, your conversations will be spicy. Erotically tinged compliments, wishes, and remarks make each of you feel special and aroused.

Experimenting with new positions — as well as locales — for lovemaking, and enhancing your pleasures with lotions, massage oils, and other accessories will be mutually satisfying. Watching movies

with sensuous themes will be satisfying too. Because you experience touching and stroking so intensely, these bring joy to your relationship. Depending on your individual levels of Emotional Intensity, sex can even transport you to ecstatic closeness.

Your biggest challenge? To value your physical passion together as important but not as the raison d'etre of your relationship. For no matter how much you enjoy each other sensually, you'll need to cultivate additional areas of shared interest and activity. Let your libidinous zest and zeal flow into other dimensions of your life as a couple.

You Both Score Low

You two definitely have little interest in the touchy-feely world. Human life offers so many interesting things to learn and experience that to you, highly sexed people really seem to have a big problem. The actress Mae West may have immortalized the suggestive line "Come up and see me sometime," but men and women who actually find that sentiment worth repeating — and far worse, worth emulating — leave you both totally cold.

As a couple, you find ways to express your caring and interest for each other that have little focus on your bodies. The thought of being frequently touched, hugged, squeezed, and groped by your partner is a definite turnoff. A light kiss is usually sufficient to gladden your heart. For you, the act of raising the physical heat too often is antithetical to the wise saying that "more is less."

It's certainly not necessary for you as a pair to make love often, or to experiment with sex in different positions and settings, for you to feel happy about your relationship; affection definitely means other things. And as for looking at erotic art or watching steamy films together, acting out sexual fantasies by role-playing with toys and props, or swinging in threesomes and

---

GREAT EXPECTATIONS

- If your partner is high on Libido, expect lots of touching and sexy behavior.
- If your partner is low on Libido, expect to hear, "Maybe later" fairly often.

foursomes, all that is one big sordid garbage heap for you guys. It's about as enticing as taking a swim at your city's sewage plant.

While dressing well and looking good may certainly be your mode, you'll both prefer respectable styles that leave a lot to the imagination. It's likely that you've felt this way at least since early adolescence. Likewise, there will be little worry in your bond

WHAT YOUR PARTNER LIKES TO HEAR

• If he or she is high on Libido, say, "Come over here and let me kiss you."

about sexual straying — for neither of you gets easily sensually attracted and aroused by people you meet. Affairs aren't impossible, of course, but you two are much less prone to them than other couples.

Your greatest challenge as a couple? To let your libidinal impulse tiptoe gently into your life from time to time. This can be done, for example, by watching movies not with pornographic content but with love as the major theme. In sharing all the pleasures of your rich lives together, your sexuality will be like a twist of lime in your cool, delicious drink.

You Score High, but Your Partner Scores Low

Be forewarned: You're going to feel sexually frustrated a lot. Indeed, many therapists who treat couples in conflict see discord on this trait as essentially insurmountable — a greater obstacle to lasting intimacy than discord over any other trait, with the sole exception of Idealism. Almost daily, or close to it, you're going to want sensual touching, caressing, and lovemaking, but your partner will not share your passion.

You're understandably likely to feel hurt, upset, and rejected, but don't try to "psychoanalyze" or "psychologize" your partner's lack of sexual or physical interest. How do we mean this?

WHAT RUFFLES YOUR PARTNER'S FEATHERS

- If your partner is high on Libido, she gets ruffled when deprived of frequent romantic touching and sex.
- If your partner is low on Libido, he gets ruffled by frequent displays of sensuality.

To put it simply, the desire for much touching and sensuality just isn't in his or her emotional makeup. Know well: This disinterest isn't intended to demean, belittle, or insult you — and your partner most definitely isn't secretly nursing a rising eroticism that will one day burst forth into your life together.

More than just feeling ignored in your libidinous needs, you're also likely to view your partner as a prude. You enjoy hearing spicy jokes and stories, watching erotic movies, and experiencing the entire realm of sexuality as a natural and exuberant aspect of life. But not your partner, who's more likely to be annoyed or even offended by your attraction to this domain.

Be aware that your partner most likely feels badly misperceived and misunderstood. Nobody likes to feel falsely accused. His or her love for you may truly be as wide as the proverbial sky, but the desire for frequent touching and sensual play just isn't there. It's unnatural to your partner's way of being in the world, and if he or she is expected day after day to match your zeal for such activity, resentment is sure to arise. Such disagreement is bound to spill over into other areas of your life together.

You Score Low, but Your Partner Scores High

Pills and herbal remedies designed to heighten sagging libido at all ages are today's global pharmacological and Internet rage, but let's be honest here: Though an envious number might rate you *lucky* to have your particular relationship problem, you'd rather see a medicinal product to slow down your partner's sensual urge, not give it an additional boost. For on an everyday basis, his or her surging sexual drive is something you'd definitely like to see lessened.

Intimacy to you doesn't demand or require constant physical touching, foreplay, or lovemaking. In your emphatic view, life offers so many wonderful ways to share close feelings — so many different kinds of shared pleasurable activities — that sexuality is clearly overrated. While you certainly don't consider yourself a prude, it's far more important for you to experience love in other ways besides erotically.

However, your partner sees things differently. And while discord on any of the Big 12 traits creates relationship hassles, conflict over Libido is among the sharpest

> ### EXPRESSING AFFECTION: GIFT-GIVING AND COMPLIMENTS
>
> When your partner is high on Libido:
> - Give sexy lingerie or briefs.
> - Compliment his or her touch and lovemaking technique.

and most uncompromising. You're going to feel constantly pressured, disturbed, and even invaded and demeaned by his or her insistence on frequent sex and stimulation. You're likely to feel sexually used, and that your partner is adolescent and shallow, or even perverse, with a "one-track mind" and kinky tastes. And even when you sincerely — and as gently as possible — decline his or her libidinous advances, expect lots of sulking and hostile accusations about your emotional coldness and its causes.

When you're out together, you're often going to feel offended by your partner's flirtatious behavior as well as hurt and rejected by his or her admiring looks and comments about others' attractiveness. Your partner's frequent masturbation and enjoyment of sexual jokes, movies, and Internet pornography will also leave you feeling disturbed and alienated.

Don't kid yourself. If you think that your partner is just "going through a temporary phase due to stress" or will "outgrow" such behavior, or that libido in a love relationship can be easily replaced by other aspects, think again. Men and women at age twenty, fifty, and eighty differ significantly in their sensual intensity. If you already see a big discrepancy between you two on this trait, know that its effect will only intensify as time passes. You'll also face the increasing possibility of affairs. From all evidence, this particular chasm cannot be bridged.

CHAPTER NINE

NURTURANCE

"**T**here's just something about a teddy bear that's impossible to explain," writer James Ownby reminisced. "When you hold one in your arms, you get a feeling of love, comfort and security. It's almost supernatural."[1]

Does such sentiment make you feel warm and happy? As you think nostalgically about bygone days, do memories of beloved stuffed animals or real-life birds, dogs, cats, fish, lizards, and myriads of other pets dance merrily in your mind's eye? If you really try, can you recall all their names — those you lovingly held and fed, bathed and walked, and treated as though they were your own offspring? Would you agree that your life was marvelously enriched by all that gentle caregiving?

---

1   Helen Exley, ed., *Teddy Bear Quotations* (New York: Exley Publishing, 1990).

Or does this whole "warm and fuzzy" realm encompassing childhood teddy bears and pets and caring for others in general seem foreign to your hard-edged sensibility? Do you basically expect people, however important in your life, to care for themselves, to stand on their own two feet, and definitely to allow you to do the same?

Such questions revolve around the Big 12 trait known as Nurturance, involving our tendency to bestow care on others. Though of major importance in love relationships, it's rarely mentioned, much less highlighted, as a factor that either brings partners closer together or pushes them apart. Those high on Nurturance are inspired by the heroic actions of historical figures like Florence Nightingale, Albert Schweitzer, and Mother Teresa.

Known as the "Lady with the Lamp" during the horrific Crimean War between England and colonial South Africa in the late nineteenth century, nurse-activist Nightingale not only cared for thousands of gravely injured soldiers, but she also implemented hospital reforms still practiced today. Treating suffering lepers and others on the impoverished African continent, Dr. Schweitzer founded clinics and encouraged countless people to enter the medical field as a powerful way to give of themselves. Mother Teresa devotedly toiled for decades as a missionary in India, giving hope and sustenance to those who felt almost wholly abandoned in their poverty and illiteracy.

Vocational psychology indicates that highly nurturing people are likely to be found in specific careers including nursing, teaching, guidance counseling, and social work. Traditionally, of course, these have been stereotyped as "feminine" occupations. However, there's no personality evidence that women are inherently more nurturing than men. This is especially true when it comes to day-to-day intimacy: Those who delight in caring for pets and plants, who have warm childhood memories of teddy bears, and who embrace pampering in their relationship can well be found in both genders.

EARLY SIGNS

Psychologists long believed that infants had little emotional life or showed any true signs of an innate personality, except for their Activity Level. But current research has dispelled that myth. It's now clear that babies exhibit the trait of Nurturance in simple form: As young as just a few months old, some infants instantly become upset and cry when they see their caretaker, parent, or nanny in obvious distress, such as when he or she falls or gets a cut. Experimentally, researchers also find that preschoolers differ widely in their reaction to videos or stories depicting animals or humans in danger. While some youngsters are highly concerned about the character's plight — "Mommy, will Flipper be all right?"— others are blithely indifferent. By the time most children reach kindergarten, virtually all teachers and parents can readily identify those who delight in growing seedlings, petting puppies, befriending stray cats, and worriedly trying to rescue fallen birds with broken wings. Likewise, in any elementary school classroom, some will unhesitatingly reach out and hug a sobbing classmate, whereas many others will not.

By adolescence, those high on Nurturance are likely to serve as peer tutors, camp counselors, or volunteers in animal shelters, hospitals, and nursing homes. They also may be active in school or community gardening projects, where having a "green thumb" is a decided asset.

BEYOND STEREOTYPES

It's often assumed mistakenly that Nurturance and Need for Companionship are almost interchangeable — or even synonymous — but that's definitely false. Caring attentively for pets or houseplants is not the same as sharing intimate dreams, hopes, and longings with a beloved. While millions talk to their poodles, Siamese cats, or parakeets, the conversation usually isn't reciprocal. Conversely, many persons who lack the impulse to pamper and who regard pets as bothersome nevertheless enjoy daily soul-baring talk.

SELF-QUIZ ON NURTURANCE

Please read each question carefully and mark the one answer that best fits you. There are no right or wrong answers, and you need not be an "expert" to take this quiz. Describe yourself honestly and state your opinions as accurately as possible. Be sure to answer each item. If you make a mistake or change your mind, erase your answer completely. Then mark the number that corresponds to your correct answer.

- Mark a 1 next to the statement if it's *definitely false* or if you *strongly disagree.*
- Mark a 2 next to the statement if it's *mostly false* or if you *disagree.*
- Mark a 3 next to the statement if it's *about equally true or false,* if you cannot decide, or if you are *neutral* on the statement.
- Mark a 4 next to the statement if it's *mostly true* or if you *agree.*
- Mark a 5 next to the statement if it's *definitely true* or if you *strongly agree.*

_____ 1. I've always enjoyed taking care of animals.

_____ 2. I dislike having to depend on other people when I get sick.

_____ 3. Too many parents sacrifice themselves needlessly for their kids.

_____ 4. Gardening is one of my favorite activities.

_____ 5. People need to take care of themselves instead of depending on others.

_____ 6. I enjoy feeding pigeons in the park.

_____ 7. I like to pamper someone I love.

_____ 8. I would resent taking care of someone's pets while they were away.

_____ 9. I like to cook for guests in my home.

_____ 10. I dislike taking care of houseplants.

_____ 11. Self-sacrifice is necessary if you love someone.

_____ 12. Visiting a sick family member in the hospital is an important expression of caring for them.

_____ 13. If an elderly family member of mine couldn't live alone anymore, I wouldn't want the responsibility of their care.

_____ 14. If someone I know felt depressed, I'd go out of my way to cheer him or her up.

_____ 15. Taking care of a sick pet would disgust me a little.

_____ 16. I like to help others get something done.

_____ 17. When I see or hear a baby cry, I run to soothe them.

_____ 18. Changing a baby's wet diaper would bother me.

_____ 19. If you offer someone your finger, they are sure to want your arm.

_____ 20. I avoid having to hear people's problems.

_____ 21. Cooking for other people is a hassle.

_____ 22. I give to the homeless even when I think the money may be used for the wrong purposes.

DETERMINING YOUR SCORE

• Add the numbers you wrote by these statements: 1, 4, 6, 7, 9, 11, 12, 14, 16, 17, and 22.

Total for part A_____

• Now subtract the numbers by these statements: 2, 3, 5, 8, 10, 13, 15, 18, 19, 20, and 21.

Total for part B_____

Your score on Nurturance is A minus B:_____.

INTERPRETING YOUR SCORE

Scores on this self-test of Nurturance can range from −44 to +44.

If you scored 22 or more, then you are *high* on Nurturance. It's your nature to be a caregiver. Physically and emotionally, you like to comfort, soothe, and pamper. Who? Why, all living things, of course: plants, animals, and particularly important people in your life. When someone dear to you feels ill or troubled, your immediate impulse is to reach out and help as much as possible. In general, you expect this reaction from others too. So in the realm of intimacy, you're best suited to someone who intuits what others need for their well-being and who seeks to bestow those things.

If you scored 21 or less, then you are *low* on Nurturance. "Don't tread on me" is your viewpoint. You like to see people take personal responsibility — to meet their own needs and to care for themselves. In your view, offering a hand of support typically encourages others to shirk responsibility. Caring for plants and animals leaves you cold. And, more significant, you don't enjoy physically comforting children and adults or serving as a sounding board for their complaints. Instead, you take pride in your ability to stand on your own two feet, make independent decisions, and then carry them out without having to depend on the goodwill of others. When feeling ill or upset, you prefer to deal with it yourself. Your path to intimacy involves mutual self-respect and self-autonomy.

NURTURANCE: THE FOUR SCENARIOS

YOU BOTH SCORE HIGH

When anyone seems to be suffering, you come through for him or her, just as you do for each other. When you see a homeless person or those asking for money, your heart is moved and you give, without too much worry about whether the money will be used for some unworthy purpose: Perhaps a child is ill, perhaps they haven't eaten in days, and they are supporting a family that has been evicted, most unfairly, from their home.

> **BELIEVE IT OR NOT...**
>
> • If your partner is high on Nurturance, he likes to pamper you frequently.
> • If your partner is low on Nurturance, she prefers to let you heal yourself.

You are also attuned to each other in a very special way: Should one of you look just a little pale or cough one time too many, you are there to place your hand gently on your partner's forehead, to offer a cool drink, even to check his or her pulse. Should your partner become truly ill, you stay home from work, run to the store to buy soup and ginger ale, and are generally at their service, day and night, with jobs, friends, leisurely pursuits all abandoned for the time being.

You also share a love of taking care of plants and animals, so your home contains many of these, and you both glory in watching them grow and thrive. Your yard has plenty of trees and gardens, or if you have an apartment, you grow flowers on your patio or windowsills.

And when you bring home cat number four, your partner does not admonish you. Rather, he or she "oohs" and "aahes," especially when you say that you found the dear creature in the alley, hiding under a car, looking as if it had been abused. Any abuse of children or animals makes you furious, and you write outraged letters in protest. If the world seems at times cold and uncaring, frigid in its response to pain, you each know you can count on each other — and do. When you tell friends how your love takes care of you, they act surprised and even envious, and you recognize how fortunate you are for having found each other. Whatever you suffer, from the smallest pain to a serious injury, you feel secure that you have someone right there to help heal you. And so you are unafraid of, as Shakespeare said, "the slings and arrows of outrageous fortune," for neither the slings nor the arrows will affect you much.

Your greatest challenge? To be aware that though not all people feel the need to give as much as you do, they still make their own very worthwhile contribution to the world. And though they may not be able to give as lushly as you can, they may wish to receive all that you can give. For the world, in all its diversity, needs both givers and receivers. And both need to be equally honored as God's creatures.

You Both Score Low

"Give someone a fish, and you've helped him for a day. But teach someone to fish, and you've helped for a lifetime"

is a viewpoint that you two heartily share. For as the Bible reminds us, "God helps those who help themselves." You don't like being pampered — and you don't feel much like pampering others. More broadly, you both believe that true compassion consists of letting people stand on their own two feet and making the most of their lives. In a world filled with the immature and

IF YOU FIND YOURSELF THINKING...
• *Doesn't my partner ever enjoy comforting someone sick?* You're involved with someone low on Nurturance.
• *Doesn't my partner ever let someone sick handle their own care?* You're involved with someone high on Nurturance.

dissolute, you agree that fostering independence is the best way to be caring.

In your shared view, people need to take responsibility for their own well-being: financially, emotionally, and physically. Coddling them invariably leads first to dependency, then to weakness, and eventually to self-destructive, childlike helplessness. The results of forty years of public welfare clearly show this to you.

Individually and as a couple, you're rarely moved by people's pleas of disability or frailty, for you believe that adversity strengthens character and that greatness can arise from the humblest — and also most challenging — life circumstances. Being born poor or disabled is no excuse for expecting endless support from others: From your perspective, why deny individuals the joys of self-mastery, self-discipline, and self-actualization by doing things for them? How can they possibly grow into maturity that way? It's your conviction that the greatest happiness comes from being free and autonomous — and avoiding dependencies of all sorts.

> **GREAT EXPECTATIONS**
> - If your partner is high on Nurturance, expect lots of pampering.
> - If your partner is low on Nurturance, expect to take care of yourself fairly frequently.

In your life together, you'll have little desire to feed pigeons in the park, take in stray dogs or cats, raise backyard vegetables, or grow a windowsill garden. Pets and household plants just aren't your thing — and probably never were since long before you two met. More important, if one of you gets sick or fatigued, worried or depressed, the other may offer words of sincere advice but not hours of soothing talk or foot massages.

    Your greatest challenge as a couple? To be able to assess when your partner truly needs you but is reluctant to ask.

> ## WHAT YOUR PARTNER LIKES TO HEAR
>
> - If he or she is high on Nurturance, ask, "Can you give me a nice back rub now?"

Feeling he can take care of himself, he may be unwilling to burden you. But your attunement to his inner experience can and will be appreciated and will further the love you both have for each other.

You Score High, but Your Partner Scores Low

Here's a practical tip for you: Don't plan very often to get sick, very tired, or in need of tender loving care. Why? Although pampering is a wonderful part of your nature, it's definitely not of your partner's. Invariably, you'll be inclined to lavish soothing care — and you'll justifiably feel that it's not being reciprocated. Better to unabashedly nurture a pair of attentive Cocker Spaniel dog, Siamese cats or a lush flower garden than to become resentful that your partner is either ignoring you completely or exploiting you like an unpaid servant.

    When you notice that your heartfelt care is unappreciated, it's unfortunately likely that you'll begin to psychologize this unpleasant situation. You'll be tempted to speculate endlessly and to look for a million possible causes. But don't. Your partner isn't purposely mean-spirited, hurtful, or even indifferent to your well-being. Rather, he or she genuinely believes that everybody — including you — is ultimately better off standing on their own two feet and living as autonomously as possible.

Yes, you delight in pampering and being pampered, but your partner genuinely perceives that attitude as a weakness and a flaw. Consequently, your efforts at unrestrained caregiving will be repeatedly rebuffed — thanklessly and even with irritation. The more soothing and nurturing you try to be when your partner is sick, tired, or moody, the more adverse the reaction. For in your partner's perspective, your behavior is annoyingly invasive, overprotective, and smothering. "I need some space" is the reaction you'll unwittingly provoke.

You Score Low, but Your Partner Scores High

Be prepared for lots of fussing about your physical and mental health. And with your personality style, that's definitively not going to be enjoyable or even especially bearable as time goes by. For on an ongoing basis — not just when illness occasionally strikes — you're going to find what seems like your every eye blink, wince, sigh, sneeze, or cough interpreted as a sign of something worrisome and potentially serious, if not downright ominous. It's not simply that your zealously nurturing partner will insist that you see a dentist, doctor, chiropractor, therapist, acu-puncturist, or some type of "alternative healer" to maximize your wellness in regards to the most inconsequential aspect of mind or body. You'll often feel yourself considered a helpless infant or weak

---

WHAT RUFFLES YOUR PARTNER'S FEATHERS

• If your partner is high on Nurturance, she gets ruffled when deprived of someone or something to soothe.

• If your partner is low on Nurturance, he gets ruffled when given the responsibility to care for someone.

little child incapable of self-care. Though your partner, of course, won't see it this way at all, you'll be treated as frail, incompetent, or both at the same time.

But more annoyingly, you'll be expected to match this ardor for caregiving, and when you don't, you'll hear complaints and accusations about your detachment, lack of concern, and even callousness. That people grow by taking responsibility for themselves is a wise axiom that your partner won't grasp readily — or at all.

Often your partner will want to give you a back rub, a foot massage, or a bed full of fluffed-up pillows, and when you politely suggest another time, you'll be greeted with

> **EXPRESSING AFFECTION: GIFT-GIVING AND COMPLIMENTS**
>
> If your partner is high on Nurturance:
> - Give him exquisite body oils.
> - Compliment her soothing charms and back rubs.

tears or hurt feelings. Frequently too, you'll have to repeat your-self — with raised voice if necessary — that you really don't need or want such pampering.

Get ready for the bothersome presence of lots of household pets and plants in your home. You'll find it hard to fathom what motivates your partner to hug dogs on the street, take in stray cats, and spend hours painstakingly caring for flowers destined to wither and die. If you refuse to join in such activities, you'll be viewed as sterile and selfish.

"God helps those who help themselves" is among the most sensible statements you've ever heard. But don't count on your partner to embrace this philosophy any time soon. Rather, in his or her apparent view of life, we're all helpless and needy, and dependency is the glory road to happiness.

CHAPTER TEN

MATERIALISM

"**G**ood clothes open all doors," observed Thomas Fuller more than two centuries ago, echoing the old Roman adage "Clothes make the man or woman." Do you share this sentiment, typically extended to embrace ownership and enjoyment of life's finest things? Even Ralph Waldo Emerson, the most celebrated philosopher of United States history, seemingly did so; for amidst all his emphasis on transcendence and self-realization, he wryly admitted, "The sense of being well-dressed gives a feeling of inward tranquility which religion is powerless to bestow."

Comprising fashion consciousness, trendiness, and a taste for what's chic, the Big 12 trait we'll discuss in this chapter is known as Materialism. While certainly exerting influence in the business world — though the "dressed-for-success" approach was overhyped in our opinion — it's in the realm of romantic intimacy that this trait really has power. Materialism is important not only during the period of initial attraction and of first dates but also in subsequent stages of romance. For this reason, we're often surprised how frequently it's overlooked by relationship advisors and counselors.

It's crucial to distinguish this trait from both Aestheticism and Idealism. Many people who enjoy music or art — even avidly play an instrument or draw — like to hunt for bargains and dress simply. Frumpy and the antithesis of fashionable, they're easy to spot in museums or concert halls. No, they're not trying to look casual or to "dress down," but, rather, they are oblivious to everything trendy — and are often proud of it. Conversely, many people who delight in being fashionable and au courant are extremely sympathetic to causes like ecology and fighting racism and poverty. Like all the Big 12 traits, Materialism is definitely independent of the others.

So where does this trait come from? Are we born with differing sensitivities to fashion and fine material things? Psychologists aren't yet sure, but the answer seems to be a tentative yes. Sensitivity to material appearance seems to play a part, as does a perceptual ability to see "gestalts" (wholes) clearly. Often parents and grandparents laugh admiringly about their three-year-old who already shows more interest in designer clothes and top-of-the-line accessories (or fancy cars and home entertainment systems) than do adult family members. Long before reaching their teenage years, such children are educating their often clueless moms and dads about fashion and all things glitzy.

EARLY SIGNS

It's clear that by age five, some boys and girls show a definite preference for fashion. Turn the clock ahead several years, and youngsters can be found immensely more knowledgeable than their parents about designer clothing and accessories, fancy cars, and even tony places to visit on family vacations. What accounts for such intriguing differences? If clearly not the result of parental training, is it all due to peer pressure and TV? Or is there a gene for fashion consciousness?

The origins of Materialism aren't yet understood definitively, but psychologists know that infants vary widely in their reactivity to bright colorful shapes or rhythmic music. Even newborns show differences in their sensitivity to moving objects, the brightness of lights, and the loudness of music. Additionally, children and teens ranking high on Materialism may be especially adept socially — not necessarily as class leaders, but in observing closely what interests and excites their peers. Our bet — and we can't prove it yet — is that this combination of factors is the best explanation for how this trait develops.

BEYOND STEREOTYPES

It's a popular idea that people high on Materialism are typically skeptical and even cynical about human nature, but there's no evidence to support it. Indeed, some of the richest men and women in the United States are very high on Idealism, giving away a good deal of their fortune to the "have-nots." Countless others who are sympathetic to social and ecological causes enjoy being fashionable and chic. Conversely, many people low on Materialism are suspicious about human nature and doing good in the world.

SELF-QUIZ ON MATERIALISM

Please read each question carefully and mark the one answer that best fits you. There are no right or wrong answers, and you need not be an "expert" to take this quiz. Describe yourself honestly and state your opinions as accurately as possible. Be sure to answer each item. If you make a mistake or change your mind, erase your answer completely. Then mark the number that corresponds to your correct answer.

- Mark a 1 next to the statement if it's *definitely false* or if you *strongly disagree.*
- Mark a 2 next to the statement if it's *mostly false* or if you *disagree.*
- Mark a 3 next to the statement if it's *about equally true or false,* if you cannot decide, or if you are *neutral* on the statement.
- Mark a 4 next to the statement if it's *mostly true* or if you *agree.*
- Mark a 5 next to the statement if it's *definitely true* or if you *strongly agree.*

_____ 1. I often daydream about being rich.
_____ 2. People who concentrate on getting rich have a big problem.
_____ 3. Living a simple life is one of my ideals.
_____ 4. I'd love to wear expensive jewelry.
_____ 5. I enjoy photo articles about the homes of rich people.
_____ 6. I'd like to drive a car that people admire.
_____ 7. I try not to own too much.

_____ 8. People who talk about money bore me.

_____ 9. I know I'd be a lot happier if I were rich.

_____ 10. I can be just as happy living in a small apartment as in a big house.

_____ 11. There are too many materialistic people in our society.

_____ 12. Keeping up with fashion is a lot of fun for me.

_____ 13. Shopping is one of my favorite activities.

_____ 14. I daydream about winning the lottery.

_____ 15. I must admit I'm a "thing" person.

_____ 16. I generally dislike people who drive fancy cars.

_____ 17. I'd like to own a big house.

_____ 18. I'm not impressed by people who dress expensively.

_____ 19. I could care less what kind of car someone drives.

_____ 20. People who like to shop as a hobby seem shallow to me.

_____ 21. Magazine articles about fancy houses annoy me.

_____ 22. I like dining at expensive restaurants.

DETERMINING YOUR SCORE

- Add the numbers you wrote by these statements: 1, 4, 5, 6, 9, 12, 13, 14, 15, 17, and 22.

     Total for part A_____

- Now subtract the numbers by these statements: 2, 3, 7, 8, 10, 11, 16, 18, 19, 20, and 21.

     Total for part B_____

Your score on Materialism is A minus B:_____.

INTERPRETING YOUR SCORE

Scores on this self-test of Materialism can range from −44 to +44.

If you scored 22 or more, then you are *high* on Materialism. You like to dress fashionably and own things that bear the mark of luxury. Elegance and opulence are qualities that give your life zest, and you enjoy daydreaming about fancy homes and estates, expensive jewelry, chic clothing and accessories, and impressive cars. Dining at posh restaurants is likewise appealing. If you're an avid traveler, then you're undoubtedly interested in visiting glamorous resorts with wonderful conveniences. For you, intimacy with your partner involves experiencing — at least vicariously — the world's material wealth.

If you scored 21 or less, then you are *low* on Materialism. You like to live simply and unpretentiously. Keeping up with the proverbial Joneses has never been important to you. Clothing is worn to keep you comfortable and protected from the elements — not to make a fashion statement. Likewise, a car is simply a big machine meant to transport you reliably — not driven to impress people with your money and social status. You like to find bargains when you shop and dine at casual restaurants. And, if you like to travel, you prefer functional and reasonably priced hotels to the memorably lavish. For you intimacy involves sharing life's simple pleasures with someone of equal yearnings.

> ### BELIEVE IT OR NOT...
>
> - If your partner is high on Materialism, he greatly enjoys fashion, jewelry, or owning things.
> - If your partner is low on Materialism, she enjoys shopping for bargains and finding little-known dives for dining.

MATERIALISM: THE FOUR SCENARIOS

YOU BOTH SCORE HIGH

You two are certainly going to be a fashionable couple. When it comes to knowing what's chic and stylish, you enjoy a sensitivity that places you above the crowd. Since you were both small, showing off attractive clothes and other nice things you owned has been a consistent source of pleasure. Now celebrate that you've each found a partner who shares this enjoyment. Let's start with cars. You'll both want to be seen driving one that evokes admiration and envy. And you'll agree that the extra money, of course, is worth

> ### IF YOU FIND YOURSELF THINKING...
>
> - *Doesn't my partner ever like to wear anything fancy or chic?*
>   You're involved with someone low on Materialism.
> - *Must my partner have expensive tastes in everything?*
>   You're involved with someone high on Materialism.

it. After all, would you want to be known by your friends, co-workers, and neighbors as a bargain-hunter or penny-pincher? The same goes for your home: Having the right ZIP code, neighborhood, and school district is something you'll readily agree is important. It's our bet that by the time you were twelve years old, you both knew what prestige was all about.

Whether dining alone together or with friends, you'll happily choose classy restaurants. When shopping for designer clothes, accessories, home furnishings, or a myriad of other things, you and your partner have a head for the eye catching. As for vacations, they offer the best excuse of all for enjoying material things. Let others proclaim their simple tastes and price-saving triumphs with hotels, car rentals, or excursions. You both

GREAT EXPECTATIONS

- If your partner is high on Materialism, expect to become more aware of what's chic and fashionable.
- If your partner is low on Materialism, expect to hear about the latest outlet to open in your area.

know that life offers joys beyond clipping coupons and saving money by outlet-shopping for last year's styles.

Your greatest challenge? To avoid both individually and as couple becoming slaves to fashion. No matter how carefully you plan, there will be times when glitter will have to take a backseat to immediate practicality or efficiency. Don't fight it. Tomorrow is another day, and almost as surely as the sun rises, you'll both enjoy a new opportunity to dazzle others with your glitz.

YOU BOTH SCORE LOW

If you haven't already figured it out, you share a taste in simple things and avoid accumulating needless possessions. In your view, the world is filled with wanton consumption and wastefulness — not to mention sheer extravagance — so why add to it and throw away good money too? The more you two feel you are thrifty and sensible when it comes to society's seductive smorgasbord, the greater your happiness. In everyday living, you'll both enjoy finding bargains wherever they present themselves and taking advantage of cost-cutting opportunities. After all, such sayings as "A penny earned is a penny saved" and "Beware of little expenses. A small leak will sink a great ship" haven't been popular for centuries without reason. Dining at home most of the time, purchasing durable furniture, driving a practical car, staying at low-cost hotels, and certainly avoiding lavish vacations thus appeal to you as a pair.

As for keeping up with the latest chic trends, who needs it? Who cares? Undoubtedly since you were both kids, you disliked all the fuss about fancy new clothes and other material things; a set of coloring books or a solid sled were good enough. Today you're equally content to shop at outlets and obtain last year's styles at big savings. And as a couple, you heartily admit that you'd feel more than a bit uncomfortable driving a fancy car or sporting expensive jewelry, trendy sunglasses, or eye-catching suits, shoes, and accessories.

Sure as tonight's sky, it's likely that all your friends feel exactly the same way. They like to hear about bargains and live simply without all the ostentation and the tiresome need to keep up with the Joneses. Displays of fashion, status, and wealth will likewise leave them cold.

Your greatest challenge? To follow the Socratic adage "How many things can I do without?" without falling into the trap of constant self-denial. Practicality and thrift are assuredly worthwhile, but sometimes listening to your heart yields a bigger payoff in the end. Don't forget to be generous with yourself as a couple, and contentment will come.

> ## WHAT YOUR PARTNER LIKES TO HEAR
>
> - If he or she is high on Materialism, ask, "Did you see any exciting new fashions today?"

You Score High, but Your Partner Scores Low

Get ready to feel embarrassed often, for you're paired with someone whose sense of style is woeful. Probably since your junior high school days you've prided yourself on knowing what's cool to wear and own, but not so your partner. Let's be honest:

He or she was probably the one frequently teased by classmates for looking like a relic from another era. And it was youngsters like you, who best knew what was chic, who led the teasing. Now that you're both adults, do you think the fashion situation is going to be much different? Absolutely not, for our key personality traits are all highly resistant to change. You'll often find yourself disappointed and dismayed about your partner's appearance, which could so easily be improved if only he or she cared. Many times, you may even want to avoid being seen with your partner at parties or other social events, not because of personality conflicts, but because you don't want others to brand you as tacky and frumpish too.

Expect to argue a lot about expenditures. In your view, life's special pleasures are meant to be enjoyed and are worth spending money on. It's important for you to own attractive furniture and décor, to drive a fancy car, and to dine at tony restaurants. When it comes to vacations, you are certainly not concerned with how to save a few bucks on bargain accommodations but with how to bask luxuriously and memorably.

Unfortunately, your partner has a very different viewpoint — and is likely to be distressed and resentful about your willingness to cast dollars to the winds in order to be at the front of the pack in appearance and status. Depending on his or her

---

WHAT RUFFLES YOUR PARTNER'S FEATHERS

- If your partner is high on Materialism, she gets ruffled when deprived of shopping for fashionable things.
- If your partner is low on Materialism, he gets ruffled when taken shopping (even window-shopping) for what's chic.

forcefulness, you're frequently going to be challenged either openly or passively as a reckless spendthrift. Therapists know well that along with disputes about relatives and child-rearing, those focusing on money are typically the most heated and damaging to intimacy. And that's no bargain at all.

You Score Low, but Your Partner Scores High

Be prepared for dismaying news: You're paired with someone who enjoys spending money and time on being fashionable and trendy. Your dearly held values of living simply, without ostentation and pretense, are not only foreign to your partner's perspective on life, but they're hardly even respected. He or she is not merely interested in "keeping up with the Joneses" but in far outdoing them. For your partner's goal is not just to be average in style, but truly outstanding.

Get set, therefore, to argue frequently about what you spend together on big-ticket items as well as what your partner spends on his or her personal wardrobe, accessories, and latest high-tech gadgets. You'll sometimes feel furious about where your hard-earned money is going — and don't be surprised if your au courant partner eventually becomes less than forthright about purchases. In retaliation, you may be criticized for being "cheap" and a "penny-pincher." But you know that Ben

---

EXPRESSING AFFECTION: GIFT-GIVING AND COMPLIMENTS

When your partner is high on Materialism:
- Give him whatever is the latest trend in jewelry or clothes.
- Compliment his flair with fashion.

Franklin was absolutely right when he warned 250 years ago: "Beware of little expenses. A small leak will sink a great ship."

Living with a peacock will lead not only to frequent arguments about money but also to those centering on your personal appearance and frugal values. Your partner may not always state it explicitly, but you'll sense often enough his or her displeasure with your clothing, watches, jewelry, perfume, or cologne — even your hairstyle and choice of pets. For in the world of fashion, some dogs are definitely more glamorous than others!

CHAPTER ELEVEN

EXTROVERSION

Are you the life of the party? When it comes to socializing, is your philosophy "The more, the merrier?" When gatherings start getting boisterous, do you find yourself becoming increasingly excited and revved up? Is it easy for you to walk into a roomful of strangers and introduce yourself confidently to everybody? If so, you definitely show qualities associated with the Big 12 trait known as Extroversion: that is, you draw your energy from groups and from other people in general.

But if raucous gatherings typically drain you and instead you prefer solitary or one-to-one activities with a close friend, you're linked to its polar opposite, introversion. Those who are introverted are typically described as shy, reclusive, and hard to read emotionally. They exhibit the stereotypic poker face, which is inexpressive and absent of all vivid feeling.

Extroversion is among the first personality traits to be identified and measured by modern psychology's founders. Nearly a century ago, the innovative Swiss psychiatrist Carl Jung originated the term to describe people who are essentially outer directed in relation to life. Contemporary research shows that it's also perhaps the single most difficult trait to change once we reach adulthood. While an extrovert can force herself to work alone in a room for hours, it won't be at all enjoyable or inspiring. And, as soon the task is done, she'll be socializing once more around the water cooler, making jokes, bantering, and later initiating countless phone calls.

Conversely, introverts are certainly able to attend loud parties and parades, and to initiate cold sales or promotional calls on the job if absolutely required, but they'll immediately relish removing themselves from such exhausting situations as soon as the opportunity arises. Trying to turn an extrovert into someone shy and passive or an introvert into a party animal is well nigh impossible. This point has become increasingly important in understanding what contributes to romantic intimacy.

EARLY SIGNS

Extroversion ranks among the easiest personality traits to observe among infants. Between the age of two and seven months, almost all show their desire to be involved with other people: they study our faces as we talk, return our smiles, and a bit later, babble responsively to our speech. Some developmental psychologists poetically describe this pattern as baby and adult "wooing" each other.

But not all babies are the same. Certainly by the time they've reached twelve months, some clearly thrive on social attention and indeed have begun actively to elicit it with their enticing antics, facial expressions, and early words. Others, however, become uneasy, fretful, and withdrawn when faced with even a few adults around their crib. Some toddlers become highly animated in a "mommy-and-me" playgroup, whereas others are content to play alone or with a single friend. Typically by kindergarten, children are easily classifiable by teachers and parents as outgoing or shy — and the pattern generally remains consistent throughout childhood and adolescence. Increasingly, psychologists today are finding a genetic basis for both extroversion and introversion.

BEYOND STEREOTYPES

It's a prevalent misconception that extroverts are typically warm, empathic, and good listeners. For people who enjoy frequent clubbing, partying, and group activities aren't necessarily interested in cultivating close relationships with whom they meet or hang out. Think of politicians who animatedly banter and shake hundreds of hands at a campaign rally yet who never actually connect individually with anyone. Just as significant, plenty of shy and quiet people make wonderful companions in romantic intimacy or friendship. Remember, extroversion is simply a dimension of how energized or drained the presence of many people makes us feel.

SELF-QUIZ ON EXTROVERSION

Please read each question carefully and mark the one answer that best fits you. There are no right or wrong answers, and you need not be an "expert" to take this quiz. Describe yourself honestly and state your opinions as accurately as possible. Be sure to answer each item. If you make a mistake or change your mind, erase your answer completely. Then mark the number that corresponds to your correct answer.

- Mark a 1 next to the statement if it's *definitely false* or if you *strongly disagree.*
- Mark a 2 next to the statement if it's *mostly false* or if you *disagree.*
- Mark a 3 next to the statement if it's *about equally true or false,* if you cannot decide, or if you are *neutral* on the statement.
- Mark a 4 next to the statement if it's *mostly true* or if you *agree.*
- Mark a 5 next to the statement if it's *definitely true* or if you *strongly agree.*

_____ 1. Loud parties drain me.
_____ 2. I like to walk into a room full of unfamiliar people and start socializing.
_____ 3. I like to sit by myself and think or read.
_____ 4. I avoid solitary sports like swimming.
_____ 5. I would feel uncomfortable making business calls to strangers.
_____ 6. It is easy for people to read my moods.
_____ 7. Most of my friends are on the shy side.
_____ 8. I try to be the center of attention in groups.

_____ 9. I dislike dining out with a big group of people.

_____ 10. I enjoy solitary hobbies like gardening.

_____ 11. I attend outdoor events with crowds so that I can feel excitement.

_____ 12. I enjoy chatting with strangers on the bus, train, or airplane.

_____ 13. I enjoy dining alone.

_____ 14. I go to clubs to socialize.

_____ 15. I enjoy going to parties a lot.

_____ 16. Most people would describe me as a very outgoing person.

_____ 17. When I come home, I quickly go to the phone to chat with people.

_____ 18. I take vacations by myself.

_____ 19. I would rather stay home by myself than socialize at a noisy party.

_____ 20. I rarely keep my moods to myself.

_____ 21. I love returning to a quiet home and try to keep it that way.

_____ 22. At parties, I prefer to let others introduce themselves to me rather than introducing myself first.

DETERMINING YOUR SCORE

- Add the numbers you wrote by these statements: 2, 4, 6, 8, 11, 12, 14, 15, 16, 17, and 20.

    Total for part A_____

- Now subtract the numbers by these statements: 1, 3, 5, 7, 9, 10, 13, 18, 19, 21, and 22.

    Total for part B_____

Your score on Extroversion is A minus B:_____.

Interpreting Your Score

Scores on this self-test of Extroversion can range from −44 to +44.

If you scored 22 or more, then you are *high* on Extroversion. You indisputably draw your energy from being around other people. "The more, the merrier" is your motto. Loud parties and big crowds give you a wonderful boost, making you feel more alive. You enjoy initiating conversations and being the center of attention. You'll do almost anything to avoid being alone for very long. It's easy for everybody to read your emotions, so don't even try putting on a poker face. With your outgoing disposition, for you intimacy typically means bringing your partner into enjoyable group activities.

If you scored 21 or less, then you are *low* on Extroversion: that is, you're an introvert. This doesn't at all mean that you're unfriendly, simply that you draw your energy from solitude. You feel empowered when working or relaxing alone. Conversely, loud parties and big crowds leave you feeling drained and depleted. You'll avoid situations in which you need to initiate conversations with strangers or to be the center of group attention. People typically find it hard to read your facial expressions because you don't provide many clues about what you're feeling. For you, intimacy typically involves quiet, one-on-one activities.

Extroversion: The Four Scenarios

You Both Score High

You can count on it as you do tomorrow's sunrise: You two are going to be partying, clubbing, and immersed in lots of group get-togethers. Because you both enjoy meeting new people, introducing yourselves, and participating in diverse activities with others, your social network will definitely be larger — and wider — than that of other couples. You'll know many individuals through work, in your neighborhood, at the gym, and so forth. You'll have lots of friends, and you'll know all of *their* friends. For you, the more people in your life the better.

At home, you're likely to prefer company to being alone as a pair. Eating dinner with several friends or acquaintances, either at one of your homes or at an enjoyable new restaurant, is your ideal. Big social events, like weddings and graduations, will be satisfying to you both. And you'll gravitate to places where crowds congregate, whether for entertainment, sporting, political, religious, or holiday events.

> **BELIEVE IT OR NOT...**
> - If your partner is high on Extroversion, she likes constant partying.
> - If your partner is low on Extroversion, he likes reading a book quietly.

As extroverts, you are both easy to read emotionally, and this will certainly enhance your communication. Your partner won't have to guess what you're feeling: your facial expression and body language will reveal all clearly. And vice versa. Trying to hide what's going on inside runs counter to both your natures, if you try, you won't be very successful. When feeling down, both of you become energized by the presence of many others, so attending a public meeting or joining an impromptu party will quickly lift your spirits.

Your greatest challenge? Creating enough time and space during the week so that you can enjoy a "private zone" for intimacy as a couple, apart from everyone else. If you're continually surrounded by dozens of boisterous folk, deepening your relationship with your beloved can become frustratingly elusive. Make sure that you always have times to look into each other's eyes.

YOU BOTH SCORE LOW

"I want to be alone," purred actress Greta Garbo in *The Grand Hotel*, and you two can definitely emphasize. More than other couples, you're averse to clubbing, partying, and joining boisterous festivities. In a society that places an ever-increasing emphasis on being part of a team, in the workplace and elsewhere, you two stand out. But this is not to say that you're unsociable or unfriendly. In fact, many people low on Extroversion enjoy deeply satisfying friendships marked by closeness and loyalty. Particularly those with a strong Need for Companionship can bond extremely powerfully. It's simply that you both draw energy from being by yourself and feel tired and drained when plunged into a group for very long.

As a result, you'll prefer doing things alone as a couple or with someone who is equally well matched on this major trait. Thus, on Friday and Saturday evenings you are far more likely to be found at a quiet restaurant table for two or at most four rather than on a thundering dance floor packed with whooping revelers. Watching the New Year's ball fall majestically at Times Square is something you'd absolutely prefer to do together snuggling in a calm living room than "live on location,"

> ### IF YOU FIND YOURSELF THINKING...
>
> - *Doesn't my partner ever like to party?*
>   You're involved with someone low on Extroversion.
> - *Doesn't my partner ever like just being alone with me?*
>   You're involved with someone high on Extroversion.

accompanied by a million hoarsely yelling fellow celebrants. Don't expect to feel awkward turning down lots of partying and clubbing invitations; your combined introverted demeanors make it unlikely that you'll receive many. And that will suit you just fine.

Based on a lifetime of habit, you'll each often gravitate toward solitary activities — like reading, solving word puzzles, exercising while listening to music on headphones, or watching a TV program. Because introverts are typically hard to read emotionally in facial and bodily expressiveness, you and your partner may frequently find yourself thinking about the other: "He or she is really quiet tonight. Is something wrong, or it just tiredness?" Reality checks are therefore important. So speak up, ask questions, show your concern. After all, isn't that what intimacy is all about?

> ### GREAT EXPECTATIONS
> - If your partner is high on Extroversion, expect lots of interest in group get-togethers.
> - If your partner is low on Extroversion, expect lots of interest in quiet times together.

Your greatest challenge? To learn each other's subtle moods and unspoken desires for shared enjoyment — and to respond with a timely nod or smile, loving touch or chat. The extra care and attention to your partner are definitely worth it.

YOU SCORE HIGH, BUT YOUR PARTNER SCORES LOW

Don't be surprised if you often feel stifled, trapped, and confined by your partner's disinterest in group activities. You'll find it daunting to spend quiet evenings alone together instead of joining parties and social get-togethers. Initially, you'll feel surprise, and later dismay, at your partner's seeming inwardness, self-absorption, and preference for solitude.

You're likely to view your partner as aloof and perhaps even socially incompetent. You love parties — the louder the better; the more the merrier. That's who you are. But your partner will be visibly bored and unhappy, complaining of feeling tired and wanting to go home — just when you know the excitement is beginning. How will such requests make you feel? Stymied, frustrated, and put-upon.

> ### WHAT YOUR PARTNER LIKES TO HEAR
>
> • If he or she is high on Extroversion, say, "I know a great party we can attend this weekend."

Your partner is likely to see your sociability as shallow, superficial, and an avoidance of true intimacy. Remember, psychologists have found this trait among the most resistant to change in our core personalities. So any expectation you harbor that this discrepancy will eventually "go away in time" — or will be "finessed" or "smoothed over" is only wishful thinking. Someone who was an extrovert (or introvert) at age thirty-five will still be one at age eighty. So be aware: Your introverted partner is not secretly a party animal in disguise, or emotionally damaged, sulking, or trying to hurt you. He or she genuinely dislikes group gatherings and invariably feels drained in such situations. It may be hard to imagine, but your partner really thrives on solitude, lone activities like reading or swimming, or a quiet dinner with just you or with one or two others. You may feel stifled and bored by such activities, but these please and energize your partner.

You Score Low, but Your Partner Scores High

The novelist Jane Austen declared in *Emma*, "One cannot have too large a party," but that's definitely not your experience. In your view, most parties and indeed group activities are generally rather tedious affairs. Little happens there that you consider memorable or even interesting. You also find them draining and sapping of your best creative energies; the more boisterous they get, the increasingly exhausted you feel and the more eager to leave.

Unfortunately, you're paired with someone with the opposite sensibility. So get ready for lots of discord with minimal resolution. Wanting to spend time alone as a couple is your ideal; joining another is also acceptable if it's going to be a quiet evening — a movie or dinner out, or a video and delivery pizza at home. Close friendships may be important to you, and these can't possibly flower for you in boisterous, giddy settings.

To your partner, though, solitary activities with you — or joining one other couple

> ### WHAT RUFFLES YOUR PARTNER'S FEATHERS
>
> - If your partner is high on Extroversion, he gets ruffled when deprived of opportunities to hang out with friends.
> - If your partner is low on Extroversion, she gets ruffled by lots of people and crowds.

— are the epitome of dullness. No liveliness, no exuberance, no energy: He or she might as well take a sleeping pill for the evening. Your partner much prefers group merriment, and thus, let the good times roll.

the **LOVE** compatibility book

> **EXPRESSING AFFECTION: GIFT-GIVING AND COMPLIMENTS**
>
> When your partner is high on Extroversion:
> - Give her a hand-decorated serving piece.
> - Compliment his sociability.

So where does that leave you? Typically feeling ignored and rejected. If you decide to be good-natured and acceptingly "go along for the ride," boredom and fatigue will soon set in. Your partner will notice with annoyance that you're not mixing well or circulating very much. He or she may regard you as clingy and dependent, an albatross hung around everybody's collective neck. And however gentle or subtle your signal, your insistence on leaving will seem unfriendly and selfish. If you hold your ground and refuse to attend all such gatherings, expect to be branded by your partner's crowd as aloof and antisocial.

On the positive side, your partner is expressive, and his or her emotions are easily readable. But do remember: His or her Extroversion is here to stay.

CHAPTER TWELVE

AESTHETICISM

"Where there is music, there can be no evil," wrote Cervantes more than three hundred years ago in *Don Quixote*. Was the acclaimed Spanish writer exaggerating to make a point, or do you essentially agree? Throughout the world, many to this day would definitely support his view.

No matter what language they speak, whether they live in bustling New York or Toronto, in a quaint French village or in the Chinese countryside, those high on the Big 12 trait known as Aestheticism share an important quality. For they all count aesthetics — music, art, and nature's beauty — to be among life's greatest pleasures. "Song is the language of the angels" is a sentiment they find personally fitting.

To a degree that psychologists still find inexplicable, this commonality strikingly transcends cultural differences around the globe. It's for precisely this reason that pop performers like Elton John or U2 — or the Beatles a generation ago — captivate audiences from London to Tokyo, and that pop tunes from Brazil soon make their way to Australia, and vice versa. To those with little aesthetic drive, such phenomena seem simply the result of slick international marketing in today's mass-entertainment industry. But such a viewpoint is badly mistaken.

For one thing, it fails to explain how even young children often respond excitedly to music from vastly differing cultures: You probably remember dancing happily to Mexican songs in kindergarten, don't you? Or how lullabies and other folk tunes transcend their original time and place, inspiring people all over the world. In a very real way, globalization has made this psychological truth indisputably clear as never before.

For example, a Japanese concert pianist whom we know related that as a high school student in Yokohama, she sat down one afternoon at home to play "Danny Boy," her new assignment. Upon hearing this haunting Irish melody for the first time, her father burst into joyful tears and listened raptly. He understood nothing of the English lyrics; it was entirely the tune, transported across centuries and continents, that instantly touched his heart.

EARLY SIGNS

Psychological research shows that all infants have an inborn sensitivity to color, shape, and sound. But striking differences among them are apparent as early as their first day of life outside the womb. Some babies react eagerly — almost hungrily — to intense aesthetic stimulation, whereas others experience identical vivid colors and musical tones as unpleasant, even painful.

Because of the prevalence of musicians in certain families through the generations — from Bach and Mozart to Bob Dylan — aestheticism increasingly seems genetically influenced.

Certainly by age three to five, boys and girls high on this trait are already drawing, singing, or dancing with ardor — and often with obvious talent. By middle elementary school years, most such youngsters have eagerly begun formal study of a musical instrument, ballet, or painting. Unequivocally by adolescence, those high on Aestheticism prize their sensitivity for the joy it brings them in everyday life. By high school, whether active performers or not, they usually seek out this realm at concerts, plays, museums, and galleries above all others.

BEYOND STEREOTYPES

When it comes to the aesthetic domain — as with much of life — there are the viewers and the doers. Contrary to popular misconception, people who are high on this trait may not necessarily play an instrument, sing in a chorus, or habitually paint or draw. Rather, it's their intense enjoyment of art, music, or the beauty of nature that defines their passion. The child who stoops to sniff a flower and stands in awe before a sunset becomes a like-minded adult. Although his or her appreciation may remain focused on something external, the beautiful feeling engendered stays deliciously tucked away inside.

SELF-QUIZ ON AESTHETICISM

Please read each question carefully and mark the one answer that best fits you. There are no right or wrong answers, and you need not be an "expert" to take this quiz. Describe yourself honestly and state your opinions as accurately as possible. Be sure to answer each item. If you make a mistake or change your mind, erase your answer completely. Then mark the number that corresponds to your correct answer.

- Mark a 1 next to the statement if it's *definitely false* or if you *strongly disagree.*
- Mark a 2 next to the statement if it's *mostly false* or if you *disagree.*
- Mark a 3 next to the statement if it's *about equally true or false,* if you cannot decide, or if you are *neutral* on the statement.
- Mark a 4 next to the statement if it's *mostly true* or if you *agree.*
- Mark a 5 next to the statement if it's *definitely true* or if you *strongly agree.*

_____ 1. I am inspired by reading poetry.

_____ 2. I must admit that art museums bore me.

_____ 3. It's hard for me to relate to people who love going to classical music concerts.

_____ 4. Sometimes while looking at a sunset or the ocean, I feel intense joy.

_____ 5. The beauty of my home is important to me.

_____ 6. I enjoy listening to new musical releases.

_____ 7. I am fascinated by books of art or photography.

_____ 8. Poetry and literature bore me.

_____ 9. I enjoy going to art galleries.

_____ 10. Looking at a sunset or at the sky does not move me.

_____ 11. I sometimes cry when listening to beautiful music.

_____ 12. Buying musical CDs seems like a waste of money.

_____ 13. Music is nice, but I don't feel it intensely.

_____ 14. Going to the ballet or opera would bore me.

_____ 15. I definitely would not want to spend my Saturday afternoon at an art gallery.

_____ 16. To me, music is a spiritual experience.

_____ 17. I never feel awed when looking at a landscape.

_____ 18. I feel enchanted by the architecture of old buildings.

_____ 19. Most of my friends have little interest in art or music.

_____ 20. I often paint or take photographs as a hobby.

_____ 21. Listening to music is one of my favorite activities.

_____ 22. I don't get excited looking at flowers, trees, or landscapes.

DETERMINING YOUR SCORE

- Add the numbers you wrote by these statements: 1, 4, 5, 6, 7, 9, 11, 16, 18, 20, and 21.

    Total for part A_____

- Now subtract the numbers by these statements: 2, 3, 8, 10, 12, 13, 14, 15, 17, 19, and 22.

    Total for part B_____

Your score on Aestheticism is A minus B:_____.

INTERPRETING YOUR SCORE

Scores on this self-test of Aestheticism can range from −44 to +44.

If you scored 22 or more, then you are *high* on Aestheticism. You enjoy art, design, music, poetry, and literature — or the beauty of nature — deeply. Such experiences fill your being with delight, and a life empty of these moments would truly feel lackluster. It would be hard for you to imagine happiness apart from aesthetic encounters. People who share this sensitivity are your "birds of a feather." Intimacy for you is forged in heartfelt appreciation of musical and artistic experiences.

If you scored 21 or less, then you are *low* on Aestheticism. This doesn't mean that artistic and musical experiences may not be pleasing, only that your deepest joys originate elsewhere. Although you may certainly like particular songs, works of art, or scenic vistas, they're not emotionally overwhelming to you. They don't knock you off your feet. Rather, your soul gets its fulfillment from the many other avenues that life offers. As for intimacy, it's likewise sustained by different sorts of shared joys than the purely aesthetic.

> ## BELIEVE IT OR NOT...
>
> - If your partner is high on Aestheticism, she often feels starved for music or art.
> - If your partner is low on Aestheticism, he gets little enjoyment from art, music, or nature's beauty.

AESTHETICISM: THE FOUR SCENARIOS

YOU BOTH SCORE HIGH

You two will experience lots of happiness enjoying beauty together. Whether your focus individually or as a couple is on music, art, photography, film, or nature's splendor, expect many lasting benefits: appealing settings like museums and concert halls, stimulating conversations, and of course, good times. It's our experience that Aestheticism can be a very strong bonding force for couples.

At home, both of you value a beautiful environment. No, this doesn't necessarily mean that you'll be lavishing dollars on interior decoration, original artwork and sculpture, and other fancy furnishings — whether you do will depend on how prominent is Materialism in your personalities. Rather, your aesthetic bent signifies that you'll both agree readily — and largely instinctively — that your home must provide a sense of daily beauty and harmony.

It won't be necessary for you to convince your partner that money spent on artwork, pottery, musical CDs, concerts, or sight-seeing trips is important to your happiness. While his or her particular aesthetic tastes and interests may certainly vary from yours — and you don't really want a clone, anyway, right? — your partner knows from personal experience just how satisfying these elements are in making your days truly worthwhile. Absolutely count on it: from early childhood to now, each of you has resonated strongly with aesthetic beauty and will surely continue to desire its delights in your lives together.

Your greatest challenge? To accept as a couple that many men and women you'll meet will share virtually none

> ### IF YOU FIND YOURSELF THINKING...
>
> - *Does my partner always have to be so absorbed in music?*
>   You're involved with someone high on Aestheticism.
> - *Doesn't my partner ever enjoy looking at beautiful art?*
>   You're involved with someone low on Aestheticism.

of your pleasure when it comes to Aestheticism. You'll each need to see your aesthetic ardor in perspective: as wonderful and exhilarating but ultimately as one among many paths to a soulful enjoyment of life.

You Both Score Low

"All art is quite useless," Oscar Wilde once quipped, and you two would definitely agree. Rhapsodizing endlessly about delightful music, painting, sculpture, or staged performance is foreign to your experience of what's really important in life. It's clear that some people claim to have wonderful, deeply meaningful, and even blissful moments while gazing at a French watercolor of cherries or hearing a Mozart piano sonata, but that's never been the case for you.

It's likely that you've each felt this way since long before high school. In fact, we'd lay odds on the fact that art and music classes bored you to proverbial tears and were among your least favorite subjects. Yes, you agree intellectually with the statement that "it takes all kinds to make a world," but frankly, you've both often wondered how people can possibly waste their precious weekend and holiday time tramping through art museums and galleries, gaping at opera and ballet, sitting through plays and art-house movies, or traveling long distances just to look at a sunset, mountain view, or a three-hundred-year-old Italian plaza.

> ### GREAT EXPECTATIONS
>
> - If your partner is high on Aestheticism, expect to experience more art and music.
> - If your partner is low on Aestheticism, don't expect an interest in attending concerts and museums.

It all just seems more than a bit tedious and pretentious to you both, and you'll definitely choose friends who feel the same way. Like you, they'll enjoy a wide range of interests and activities apart from the aesthetic and will be equally disinclined to spend time and money on operas and museums. As a couple, you'll absolutely be more concerned with your home's comfort and maintenance, up-to-date appliances, neighborhood, and proximity to work and acquaintances than with its architectural or interior dazzle. Likewise, you'll share an antipathy for those who want to impress relatives, co-workers, and neighbors with their artsy knowledge and travels. For you, hanging around people like that is about as exciting as going to the dentist.

> ### WHAT YOUR PARTNER LIKES TO HEAR
>
> • If he or she is high on Aestheticism, ask, "Have you heard any good music lately?"

Your greatest challenge as a couple? To venture into aesthetic venues like museums to enlarge your social sphere, for some of the interesting people you meet will also have wandered this foreign domain. Take guidance from the adage "It's a great place to visit, but I wouldn't want to live there." A visit is just a visit, but who knows? Something related to your other traits may just beckon you back.

You Score High, but Your Partner Scores Low

Gird yourself to feel a formidable gap between your daily ardor for music and art versus your partner's lack of responsiveness. Often you'll want to share your excitement for the new musical CD you've bought and ask your partner immediately to listen —

but he or she won't be eager at all. The latest, well-reviewed films will entice you, but definitely not your partner. You'll start making plans to see a new gallery or museum exhibition in your locale, but your partner will find such activities a crashing bore.

Indeed, don't be surprised to find that your desire to attend opera, ballet, or a world music concert is greeted with complete disinterest and even annoyance. To your partner, such venues are as appealing as reading a computer manual would be for you.

In everyday life, you'll be inspired to comment on beautiful sunsets, afternoon skies with majestic clouds, and interesting archi-

> ### WHAT RUFFLES YOUR PARTNER'S FEATHERS
> - If your partner is high on Aestheticism, he gets ruffled when deprived of art, music, or nature's beauty.
> - If your partner is low on Aestheticism, she gets ruffled when expected to attend artistic or musical events.

tectural details that you notice. But your partner will be unmoved and likely to find your remarks irrelevant to life's practical matters, if not downright repetitive and pretentious.

Just remember: Your partner isn't harboring someone inside who actually thrives on music and art and is intentionally indifferent, emotionally rejecting, or hurtful for reasons unknown. Your intense reaction to aesthetics — in all its dazzling forms — just isn't in his or her personality makeup. No matter how sincere or eloquent your descriptions, the attraction simply isn't there.

YOU SCORED LOW, BUT YOUR PARTNER SCORES HIGH

When the British essayist William Congreve memorably declared three hundred years ago, "Music has charms to soothe a savage breast," he was living, after all, in a time when science was still quite primitive. Many people still believed that the sun revolved around the earth and that the world was flat. So in your view, he could easily be forgiven for expressing such silly sentimentality, however poetic it may be. But unfortunately for your relationship, you're paired with a twenty-first-century inhabitant who considers aesthetic experiences the be-all and end-all of life.

> ### EXPRESSING AFFECTION: GIFT-GIVING AND COMPLIMENTS
>
> When your partner is high on Aestheticism:
> - Give her a CD or an art calendar.
> - Compliment his good taste in music or art.

So get ready. Expect to be dragged around a lot to museums, art galleries, scenic vistas, or concerts that dreadfully bore you — or to be constantly defending your refusal to waste valuable time on such unsatisfying and pretentious activities. When you truthfully explain, as good-naturedly and gently as possible, that musical and artistic events simply leave you cold, your partner will react with disbelief and annoyance. Depending on where you rank on Emotional Intensity, nerves may fray and tempers fly. As the sheer number of such conversations increases, do you think you'll feel closer or more distant from one another?

You're likely to be criticized often for lacking good taste — or for "following the crowd" — when it comes to selecting home décor and furnishings. Even if you willingly spend a big chunk of money to adorn walls, furniture, and cabinets, your partner frequently will find fault with the aesthetic excellence of your preferences. You may find it hard to escape too from the constant presence of loud music.

It's almost certain that your partner and his or her like-minded friends will regard you as boorish when it comes to conversing about culture. Sure, they may be polite enough to your face, but behind your back, your disinterest in music, art, and related fields such as theater, dance, photography, and architecture will cause them to view you as a backwoods denizen or a Neanderthal.

CHAPTER THIRTEEN

ACTIVITY

LEVEL

Do you believe that when it comes to life, "The race is to the swiftest" or conversely, "Slow and steady wins it all"? Do you feel surrounded most of the time by slowpokes and sluggards, or by those dashing by too quickly ever to enjoy their days? It's eminently clear that people differ strongly from one another on the Big 12 trait known as Activity Level. For some of us prefer awakening quickly and plunging into a whirl of daily accomplishment, while others prefer a more relaxed and mellow lifestyle.

What about you? Because work responsibilities and pressures in an increasingly competitive global market affect us all, psychologists find that a far better indicator of your standing with regard to this important personality trait is how you typically spend your leisure, especially vacation, time. Does the thought of a wonderfully free weekend immediately evoke images of backpacking, cycling, skiing, tramping through museums and galleries, and browsing interesting shops — or of sleeping late and lounging comfortably as the hours idly pass?

When you arrive at your hotel, is your impulse to leave your suitcases by the bed and start seeing new things immediately? Or would you rather plop onto the bed, kick off your shoes, and sink into a luxurious rest? Of course everyone has both tendencies at least occasionally. But generally people differ in their preferred levels of activity — regardless of their age. If you were super-active in your youth, there is a good chance you will continue as you age and vice versa. The older marathon runner did not suddenly become a sports enthusiast. Nor did the older couch potato suddenly become sedentary. Our traits determine our preferences and these traits are apparent when we first enter this world.

Whatever your predilection in terms of activity, we're sure it's been vital to your personality since childhood. Indeed, it's one of the Big 12 traits most closely linked biologically to temperament and least influenced by parental and cultural values. Indisputable evidence has now amassed that even within the same family, siblings often differ widely from birth onward in their degree of activity. So when it comes to romantic compatibility, be aware that major personal change involving this trait is unlikely.

EARLY SIGNS

Activity Level is one of our most basic core personality features. Not only infants but also newborns differ widely on how much time they typically sleep — and engage in head-turning, sucking, and intent looking. This pattern continues throughout childhood. As every parent knows, some youngsters enjoy daily napping and resting, and easily prepare for bedtime. Others, however, almost never nap or rest, and putting them to bed often provokes a prolonged battle.

At age five, highly active girls and boys will spend lots of time playing with their toys, running around the playground, and playing games or sports. As preteens, highly active boys and girls continue with their busy lives: Now it is organized soccer, baseball, bowling, tennis, or whatever their tastes dictate. By age fourteen, both sexes are more sophisticated, and while sports are still important, activities may now also include rock climbing or ballet lessons. Those active in childhood and adolescence are likely to stay active, while those more sedentary remain so.

Beyond Stereotypes

Contrary to popular belief, people who rank high on Activity Level aren't necessarily athletic or even interested in sports. Rather, the trait entails one's preference for waking quickly, keeping rests and naps to a minimum, and doing things all day long. Such individuals may not be well coordinated or athletically inclined, but they will show little daily desire to lounge and sleep.

SELF-QUIZ ON ACTIVITY LEVEL

Please read each question carefully and mark the one answer that best fits you. There are no right or wrong answers, and you need not be an "expert" to take this quiz. Describe yourself honestly and state your opinions as accurately as possible. Be sure to answer each item. If you make a mistake or change your mind, erase your answer completely. Then mark the number that corresponds to your correct answer.

- Mark a 1 next to the statement if it's *definitely false* or if you *strongly disagree.*
- Mark a 2 next to the statement if it's *mostly false* or if you *disagree.*
- Mark a 3 next to the statement if it's *about equally true or false,* if you cannot decide, or if you are *neutral* on the statement.
- Mark a 4 next to the statement if it's *mostly true* or if you *agree.*
- Mark a 5 next to the statement if it's *definitely true* or if you *strongly agree.*

_____ 1. I must admit that I'm something of a "couch potato."

_____ 2. I prefer a quiet weekend at home.

_____ 3. Even when I'm not working, I like to get up early and get things done.

_____ 4. My ideal vacation involves a lot of activity, like backpacking or sight-seeing.

_____ 5. I like taking naps often.

_____ 6. Compared to most people my age, I like a slow pace of life.

_____ 7. I get physically restless easily.

_____ 8. I often daydream about lying on the beach all day and just relaxing.

_____ 9. I like to sleep late on weekends.

_____ 10. To me, a foreign vacation would involve too many hassles to be really enjoyable.

_____ 11. I must admit that sometimes I find it hard to slow down.

_____ 12. I'm not really happy unless I'm doing things.

_____ 13. I avoid spending time lounging at home.

_____ 14. I like physically active recreations like jogging, dancing, or hiking.

_____ 15. Most people consider me highly active.

_____ 16. I find it hard to relate to people who always need to be doing something.

_____ 17. Being around very active people is fun for me.

_____ 18. The idea of a leisurely breakfast in bed certainly appeals to me.

_____ 19. I prefer to spend my vacations doing relaxing things, like lounging by a pool.

_____ 20. I generally dislike napping unless I'm sick.

_____ 21. Nobody who knows me well would call me hyperactive.

_____ 22. Sometimes I have so much energy I don't know what to do with it.

DETERMINING YOUR SCORE

- Add the numbers you wrote by these statements: 3, 4, 7, 11, 12, 13, 14, 15, 17, 20, and 22.

    Total for part A_____

- Now subtract the numbers by these statements: 1, 2, 5, 6, 8, 9, 10, 16, 18, 19, and 21.

    Total for part B_____

Your score on Activity Level is A minus B:_____.

Interpreting Your Score

Scores on this self-test of Activity Level can range from −44 to +44.

If you scored 22 or more, then you are *high* on Activity Level. You always seem to be on the go. To feel truly alive, you need to be doing things. It's enjoyable to get up early and immediately start the day on the right track by accomplishing something. You shun naps and long nights of sleep and really don't see the point in taking time out to rest. It's hard to feel close to those with a sedentary disposition; life seems to be passing them by. For you intimacy with your partner invariably involves lots of shared activity.

If you scored 21 or less, then you are *low* on Activity Level. You enjoy experiencing life in a relaxed way. "Slow and steady wins it all" and "Haste makes waste" are your mottos. You dislike being rushed and pushed into high gear. To be expected to engage in constant activity is a definite turnoff. You prefer lounging at home to energetic venturing, and you like keeping company with people who don't seem driven or frenetic in any way. As for intimacy, savoring small, slow moments with your partner comes much more naturally than sharing energetic endeavors.

ACTIVITY LEVEL: THE FOUR SCENARIOS

You Both Score High

Life is full of surprises, but one thing is certain: You two are going to be busy a lot. Doing things not only appeals to both of you, it's also who you are on the deepest level. In contrast to couples who can't wait to sleep late on weekends and who lounge away the hours blissfully at home, your ideal is to get up early and go. The two of you accomplish many things together. The more you're hiking or bicycling, visiting distant friends or relatives, sight-seeing or traveling to exotic locales, the happier you feel.

Almost instinctively, both of you share an aversion to the sedentary way of life. Basically, home for you is a place to hang your proverbial hat, or maybe your new running shoes. Sure, like everyone else you want a comfortable place to sleep at night, but little else about your domicile is really vital to your sense of well-being. Indeed, for couples like you, having easy access to public transportation or major highways is probably more important than being able to "nest" contentedly.

Viewing your residence as essentially a place for sleep and departure, neither of you desires to invest much personal energy, time, or money in matters like home improvement or restoration. Rather, spending money on athletic activities, wilderness trekking, or journeying definitely seems

> **BELIEVE IT OR NOT...**
>
> - If your partner is high on Activity Level, she likes to be active and to accomplish a lot.
> - If your partner is low on Activity Level, he really likes staying at home.

more appealing. Unless either you or your partner is specifically interested in carpentry or a related craft, don't expect your living space ever to look very different from how it was when you first moved in.

Finding things to do every day, weekend, and vacation will fill your relationship with shared purpose and satisfaction. When the stars come out at night you may feel tired — even exhausted — but nonetheless you will feel delighted about how much you jointly accomplished within the fixed constraint of only twenty-four hours each day. Conversely, feeling that you've wasted time "doing nothing" leaves both of you frustrated and regretful.

Your greatest challenge? Truly allowing a sense of home and its blessedness to fill your life together. If you can accept — even embrace — this sacred awareness as an active couple, you've got it made.

You Both Score Low

"When I was home, I was in a better place" is a line from Shakespeare's *As You Like It* that resonates wonderfully with you two. In a world that seems to you obsessed with marathon runners, dancers, and trailblazers of every stripe, it's nice to know that the Bard exactly understood your sensibility.

As a couple, you're definitely happiest when lounging in your cocoon. The living room couch is your kingdom, and you like it that way. No inducement to change will prove convincing, for what could make you two give up such daily comfort and pleasure together? Let others chase wild lions across African plains on safari vacations, tame galloping horses on dude ranches, or climb Mount Everest in the

> ### IF YOU FIND YOURSELF THINKING...
>
> - *Doesn't my partner ever slow down?*
>   You're involved with someone high on Activity Level.
> - *Doesn't my partner ever get off the couch?*
>   You're involved with someone low on Activity Level.

winter. You know in a way such personalities never will revel the incomparable delights and joys of domesticity.

When socializing with friends and relatives, you'll prefer staying at home, enjoying delivery pizza or a backyard barbecue, to venturing into the hassles of traffic and restaurant waiting lines. And why go through all the draining fuss of getting to a theater just to see something that will come out on home video in just a few weeks? As for weekends, you both relish rest and relaxation. "Whoever invented breakfast in bed should win the Nobel Peace Prize" is a sentiment that warms your hearts.

As for vacations, sipping a delicious drink while on a chaise lounge at a resort hotel swimming pool or cruise-ship deck is probably as close to your version of heaven as it gets. Wilderness backpacking and cycling, day-after-day sight-seeing in exotic foreign cities may appeal to some folk, but not to you. The more time to lounge, and the deeper the lounging, the better you two will feel together.

GREAT EXPECTATIONS

- If your partner is high on Activity Level, expect lots of interest in doing things outside the home.
- If your partner is low on Activity Level, expect lots of interest in cocooning at home.

Your biggest challenge as a couple? To overcome your pleasure in cocooning enough to keep yourselves physically fit and reenergized by new scenes. Paddling a canoe in the nearby river, playing Frisbee in a friend's backyard, or taking a short walk in the park will strengthen your muscles and open your eyes to all of God's wonders.

You Score High, but Your Partner Scores Low

Be prepared often to feel that you're paired with a dullard and a slacker. You'll be chafing constantly at the proverbial bit from your frequent thwarted desire to see a weekday movie, go to a restaurant, or to get away somewhere, anywhere, on many weekends and holidays. Your partner will swiftly respond to such requests with pointed statements like "I'm not in the mood," "Where do you get your energy?" or simply, "I'm too tired." At best, you may hear a lot of comments like, "You go and have a good time, dear. But I'm going to stay put for the evening."

You may like to participate in sports, but your partner will have little interest in skiing, tennis, jogging, or swimming. Golf may be a reasonable compromise. As for vacations, you'll undoubtedly be ready to start exploring and sight-seeing the moment you unload your suitcases at the hotel, but your partner will prefer to "nest" there first: either comfortably sipping a poolside drink or lounging right in the room. Almost by definition, a vacation for you is a time for active enjoyment — for *doing things*. But for your partner, it's a respite from the busy world, an opportunity to rest, relax, and delightfully unwind.

> ### WHAT YOUR PARTNER LIKES TO HEAR
>
> • If he or she is high on Activity Level, ask, "Would you like to take a run together?"

Remember, your partner isn't secretly a highly active person who, for unknown psychological reasons, is suppressing this noble impulse — or worse, trying to hurt you emotionally or reject you. There are plenty of "couch potatoes" in this world, and you're mismatched with one.

You may feel increasingly stifled, thwarted, and even imprisoned at home as time goes by. But do know that your partner is no deliberate jailer and undoubtedly feels frustrated and bewildered by your seemingly constant need to be "out and about" — keeping busy from awakening to bedtime. Indeed, your partner is likely to feel ignored, dragged around, resentful, or exhausted if expected to meet your zestful day-to-day routine.

YOU SCORE LOW, BUT YOUR PARTNER SCORES HIGH

Get ready for a constant struggle to maintain your sense of well-being and relaxation. You're going to need all the support you can muster from like-minded friends and relatives, for you're going to feel like you're riding the proverbial tiger's tail every day. Why? Because your partner not only has no personal familiarity with how delicious lounging can be, but he or she finds it unfathomable as a true source of pleasure for you.

If the couch is your throne and the backyard your kingdom, you'll often feel like you're reigning alone. Don't expect much companionship either when it comes to soothing weekend mornings in bed and afternoon putterings around at home. Your partner will view all that as boring and even confining, especially compared to the delights of hiking, jogging, shopping, or pursuing aesthetic interests.

WHAT RUFFLES YOUR PARTNER'S FEATHERS

- If your partner is high on Activity Level, she gets ruffled when unable to get out and do things.
- If your partner is low on Activity Level, he gets ruffled when unable to spend leisure time at home.

You're likely to feel annoyed and hurt by your partner's demeaning attitude about your desire to make the best possible cocoon together. Instead of admiration or even agreement, you're going to hear frequent complaints like, "Don't you ever want to go out?" and "This place is starting to feel like a prison to me. Let's go somewhere, anywhere, this weekend!"

Expect to clash over home expenditures, since your partner has little interest in nesting and will instead prefer to budget for top-of-the-line sports equipment, club membership, and travel. Your dearly held plans for lovely new living room furniture, bedroom furnishings, and refurbishing projects big and small will be met with a gigantic yawn. But guess what? This may be among the only times that he or she will show a hint of sleepiness.

EXPRESSING AFFECTION: GIFT-GIVING AND COMPLIMENTS

When your partner is high on Activity Level:

- Give her a runner's outfit.
- Compliment his vitality compared to that of others his age.

CHAPTER FOURTEEN

SUBJECTIVE

WELL-BEING

How happy do you feel right now? How happy were you about an hour before you went to sleep last night? How about when you awoke this morning? Are you optimistic about the future, or do you worry a lot? Keeping in mind the old adage, do you tend to see the proverbial glass of water as half-full or half-empty?

Though seemingly simple, these questions all concern the important personality trait known as Subjective Well-Being. Psychologists have recently become convinced of its relevance to many aspects of lifestyle, including the kinds of decisions we make and even our health. As a member of the Big 12, our Subjective Well-Being also strongly impacts romantic intimacy. For almost always in daily life, individuals and couples make choices large and small flowing from their underlying emotional security and optimism.

Whether you're confident or shaky about what lies ahead, it's almost certain that you've felt this way since long before high school. The scientific evidence suggests that at an early age — perhaps soon after leaving the crib — we each acquire an internal emotional "thermostat" that sets our moment-by-moment degree of contentment. You probably never thought about it this way, but trust us: It's there. Like all the Big 12 traits, Subjective Well-Being is resistant not only to everyday ups and downs but also to major life events we experience, whether joyful or not so wonderful.

Somehow we expect that everyone reacts the same way to the same event, but it's absolutely not so. Indeed, it's precisely for this reason that newspaper articles feature super lottery winners who seem just as happy — or as miserable, as the case may be — *after* their gigantic windfall as they were *before* all those dollars spilled into their lives.

If you consider this for a moment from the standpoint of Subjective Well-Being, it makes perfect sense. For a person whose inner thermostat has been set since childhood on low contentment, coming into sudden wealth brings an onslaught of new things to worry about — from dishonest brokers and unfaithful friends to scheming co-workers and relatives. Conversely, if you already feel highly content about life moment to moment, then a huge investment portfolio is ultimately irrelevant to you.

EARLY SIGNS

We cannot ask infants whether they're optimistic or pessimistic, but, as with much of early behaviors, we can look for clues. Psychologists find that babies high on Subjective Well-Being typically tolerate well changes in daily routines, adapt to new situations with a minimum of fuss, and smile frequently rather than frowning or pouting. They're not necessarily highly outgoing or very interested in exploring their environment, but rather, these babies exude a general contentment in everyday matters like feeding, bathing, and dressing. Conversely, infants low on this basic personality trait characteristically react to changes in routine by whining or throwing a tantrum, and frequently display unhappy facial expressions.

By age five, boys and girls high on Subjective Well-Being adapt well to such major events as starting kindergarten and the birth of younger siblings. Family moves are also taken in stride. In school, such youngsters may not be class president if they're low on Extroversion, but they typically have many friends and acquaintances — as well as supportive teachers — because of their pleasant mood and acceptance of others. There's also evidence that such youngsters handle such stresses as parental divorce or illness, or an elder relative's death, more calmly than do their peers. By high school those high on Subjective Well-Being are clearly optimistic about the future, both for themselves and for the world in general. In their confident view — sometimes to the consternation of their more fretful parents— there's no point in worrying about college and the job market, because "everything will work out just fine."

BEYOND STEREOTYPES

It's a common but understandable mistake to confuse Subjective Well-Being with Idealism. However, the two traits are actually quite different. Many people are self-confident and optimistic about their own future but view human existence as a ruthless jungle where the weak fall prey to the strong. There are also plenty of altruistic people who tend to be worriers and who feel gloomy about events that may lie ahead.

SELF-QUIZ ON
SUBJECTIVE WELL-BEING

Please read each question carefully and mark the one answer that best fits you. There are no right or wrong answers, and you need not be an "expert" to take this quiz. Describe yourself honestly and state your opinions as accurately as possible. Be sure to answer each item. If you make a mistake or change your mind, erase your answer completely. Then mark the number that corresponds to your correct answer.

- Mark a 1 next to the statement if it's *definitely false* or if you *strongly disagree.*
- Mark a 2 next to the statement if it's *mostly false* or if you *disagree.*
- Mark a 3 next to the statement if it's *about equally true or false,* if you cannot decide, or if you are *neutral* on the statement.
- Mark a 4 next to the statement if it's *mostly true* or if you *agree.*
- Mark a 5 next to the statement if it's *definitely true* or if you *strongly agree.*

_____ 1. I consider myself an optimistic person.
_____ 2. On most days, I feel happy.
_____ 3. I wish I could undo a lot of things in my life.
_____ 4. I tend to hold a grudge too long.
_____ 5. I can unwind easily after work.
_____ 6. I must admit that I'm a worrier.
_____ 7. People often disappoint me.
_____ 8. I have confidence in my abilities.
_____ 9. I get along very well with my co-workers.

_____ 10. Sometimes I feel like exploding at the stupidity of others.

_____ 11. I rarely get depressed.

_____ 12. I feel that life is passing me by.

_____ 13. I seldom think about unpleasant experiences of my life.

_____ 14. Unfortunately, I've often been hurt by people I trusted.

_____ 15. I'm able to see the "silver lining" in most situations.

_____ 16. At times, I feel like a loser.

_____ 17. I know my health has gotten worse lately because of stress.

_____ 18. Thinking about the future rarely makes me tense.

_____ 19. I almost never have trouble falling asleep owing to worry.

_____ 20. I sometimes feel so stressed that I have digestive problems.

_____ 21. I don't lose my temper easily.

_____ 22. I tend to have nightmares.

DETERMINING YOUR SCORE

- Add the numbers your wrote by these statements: 1, 2, 5, 8, 9, 11, 13, 15, 18, 19, and 21.

    Total for part A_____

- Now subtract the numbers by these statements: 3, 4, 6, 7, 10, 12, 14, 16, 17, 20, and 22.

    Total for part B_____

    Your score on Subjective Well-Being is A minus B:_____.

INTERPRETING YOUR SCORE

Scores on this self-test of Subjective Well-Being can range from −44 to +44.

If you scored 22 or more, then you are *high* on Subjective Well-Being. You're one of the lucky ones, for you experience everyday living with happiness. You typically enjoy whatever you're doing at the moment without worrying about the future or ruminating about the past. From your perspective, "what's done is done" and "there's no use in crying over spilled milk." You're optimistic. For you the proverbial glass is always half-full. You rarely feel depressed, and when you do, invariably it's not for long. Nor do you get angry easily or harbor resentments against others. Life for you is indeed a "bowl of cherries." So savor them now with someone special.

If you scored 21 or less, then you are *low* on Subjective Well-Being. It's hard for you to enjoy the moment because of your worries about the future and your ruminations about the past. You think a lot about times you've been betrayed or hurt by others, and you're no stranger to vengeful fantasies. It's easy for you to feel down about your life and to berate yourself for things you should have — or should not have — done. Often when things are going well, you wonder how long they'll last before disaster strikes. If you are self-aware and accept your anxieties, then you know what to look for in your companion for intimacy.

SUBJECTIVE WELL-BEING: THE FOUR SCENARIOS

YOU BOTH SCORE HIGH

You two experience the world as a bright sunny place and probably have always done so, long before you met. Chalk it up to a secure happy childhood or perhaps to something innate; psychologists certainly aren't yet sure about this important trait. But one thing is clear: Pessimism and worrying about the future are as distant from your daily outlook as they can possibly be.

Indeed, both of you have real trouble even identifying with couples and individuals who fret a lot about things, dwell on past misfortune, or feel acutely vulnerable. You know that such people exist — you see them every day driving aggressively on the highway, waiting impatiently in post office or bank lines, or loudly arguing with store

> **BELIEVE IT OR NOT...**
>
> - If your partner is high on Subjective Well-Being, he hardly worries at all.
> - If your partner is low on Subjective Well-Being, she worries about many things, big and small.

clerks or family members. But how men and women can actually live in a constant state of anger, doubt, or gloom baffles both you and your partner.

It often seems to you both that in this wonderful world events usually turn out well if just given the chance to unfold naturally. Phrases like "don't push the river" and "go with the flow" don't seem at all hackneyed to people like you, who perennially see the glass not as half-full *or* half-empty but as filled to the brim with a delicious elixir. Whether you're talking with home repairpeople, mutual friends, relatives, co-workers, or neighbors, you instinctively feel relaxed and optimistic that everything will be fine with them all. As a pair, you don't bear grudges, nurse grievances, or dredge up the past with each other or with those outside your bond. When you contemplate your future together, you mutually bask in a warm glow.

Your greatest challenge as a couple? To understand and empathize that many people you encounter — whether because of a less fortunate childhood or genetic mix — utterly lack your easygoing disposition and faith in the future. If together you can reach out to them sympathetically rather than recoiling in shock or revulsion, your blessed sense of well-being can truly become a divine gift.

YOU BOTH SCORE LOW

For you two, life has many justifiable worries. It's filled with unpredictable, difficult, and potentially dangerous events. While some may blithely prattle on that this is the "best of all possible worlds," you two definitely would not. Let the foolish call your outlook anxious, gloomy, or simply pessimistic. In your combined experience, dating back to childhood, it's preferable rather to view it as realism. In daily living, you'll experience camaraderie by seeing the proverbial glass as half-empty. And how do you see the liquid inside the glass? The odds that it's anything very pleasant seem small to you. You each understand exactly where the other is coming from owing to your many encounters with broken promises, letdowns, and disappointments of every kind. As a couple, the issue for you isn't necessarily to be more

---

IF YOU FIND YOURSELF THINKING...

- *Doesn't my partner ever worry, get depressed, or angry?*
  You're involved with someone high on Subjective Well-Being.
- *Can't my partner stop worrying so much, or being so irritable or depressed?*
  You're involved with someone low on Subjective Well-Being.

---

orderly and to plan everything better, for you've found that detailed planning is often just as useless as taking a wild chance.

Instead, what binds you two and fortifies your days is a shared sensibility — a persistent uneasiness — that things aren't always what they seem and that they can unmistakably get a lot worse, and fast. As newspapers and the TV news make absolutely clear, all that a person has hoped and worked for can be taken away forever in a single terrible moment. Is it impolite or foolish to deny this? Does that silly Broadway jingle provide the slightest comfort when it urges us to "put on a happy face"? As a pair, you certainly don't think so.

Traveling, especially overnight, often heightens the insecurity that couples like you experience on a persistent basis, for so much can go wrong. Yet you're also well aware that most accidents occur right in the seeming safety of your home. How thoroughly these can be prevented, or even predicted, is something you both wonder about often.

> **GREAT EXPECTATIONS**
> - If your partner is high on Subjective Well-Being, expect lots of optimism about the future.
> - If your partner is low on Subjective Well-Being, expect lots of worrying and downcast moods.

Your greatest challenge as a couple is to reach out and include in your array of friends some who seem blithely unconcerned about the dark, gloomy side of life and all the bad things waiting to happen. Rather than waiting for the sun to come out before you can smile, smile anyway, for no reason at all. When the sun does appear, let its rays rejuvenate your spirit and give you a sense of blessed protection.

YOU SCORE HIGH, BUT YOUR PARTNER SCORES LOW

Get ready to spend a lot of time with someone whom you'll perceive as a worrier and a pessimist. Know also that you're likely to feel pulled down into negativity by your partner's frequent doubts and misgivings concerning the future. These worries can be about anything, from what to make for breakfast to your vacation next week to whether your two-year-old will get into a good college. Although your natural tendency is to be easygoing and genial, you've probably not been nominated yet for sainthood, right? Thus, being obliged to hear daily complaints, grudges, grievances, and disappointments is eventually going to get under your skin — and you may find yourself reacting with mounting irratability, or more likely, with emotional withdrawal.

> ### WHAT YOUR PARTNER LIKES TO HEAR
>
> • If he or she is high on Subjective Well-Being, say, "Tell me something that made you feel especially good-spirited today."

In either circumstance, your partner is almost certainly going to feel rejected. If you adopt a "benign neglect" policy of simply tuning out his or her negative moods and only responding to the positive, your partner will justifiably feel ignored. And then watch out! You will become a target for sarcasm or sadness or the latest item on his or her formidable list of gripes about life's basic unpleasantness and unfairness.

Indeed, your constant good cheer and optimism may become a particular irritant to your partner, who may misinterpret such good-naturedness as an uncaring and disinterested attitude. If you think that adopting a continually soft, soothing "there, there" demeanor toward your partner will get you out of the proverbial woods, think again — for nobody likes to feel patronized. More helpful would be to express whatever pessimism you can honestly summon, for it will be welcomed as realism and common sense.

You Score Low, but Your Partner Scores High

"An optimist is a guy that never has had much experience," declared writer Don Marquis more than a generation ago, and you staunchly agree. It's sometimes amazing to you that more doesn't go wrong in everyday life, at all levels of organizational and social order. But you're also aware that countless mishaps and crimes are never even reported, so there's definitely lots of bad news happening constantly out there. In your view, worrying about the future makes perfect sense, given the unpredictable and chaotic world we live in.

> **WHAT RUFFLES YOUR PARTNER'S FEATHERS**
> - If your partner is high on Subjective Well-Being, she gets ruffled about almost nothing.
> - If your partner is low on Subjective Well-Being, he gets ruffled by just about everything.

But somehow, your partner never sees it this way, for you're paired with someone who has probably been optimistic — and smug, in your opinion — about nearly everything since kindergarten. You might even find yourself reminded of *Mad* magazine's grinning icon Alfred E. Neuman with his adolescent answer — "What, me worry?" — to all life's crises, problems, and rocky situations.

The woods might be on fire, but instead of calling for help

and evacuating the house, your partner will be blithely toasting marshmallows — or so it will seem to you. Certainly, he or she will almost never show tension, doubt, or worry about what lies ahead.

"When life gives you lemons, it's time to make lemonade" urges an optimistic poster. But such an attitude strikes you as childish, self-indulgent, and irresponsible. There may be no use crying over spilled milk, but the sensible response is to at least clean up the mess immediately and make sure it doesn't happen again. In your view, it's hardly accidental that the lemonade poster is part of an upbeat product line touting equally smug advice about workplace problems — and juxtaposed with photos of laughing chimpanzees.

> ## EXPRESSING AFFECTION: GIFT-GIVING AND COMPLIMENTS
>
> When your partner is high on Subjective Well-Being:
> - Give her favorite candies or exotic foods.
> - Compliment his optimism and confidence.

Keep two things in mind: Your partner is not going to change on this basic personality trait, and you'll get minimal thanks or appreciation for your heartfelt concerns about your unfolding life together. Instead, you'll often be branded as depressive and downbeat, or a "worrywart." And that's something you can fruitfully ponder.

CHAPTER FIFTEEN

INTELLECTUALISM

Do you like to read for pleasure, or is it basically a chore? Does increasing your knowledge of history, science, and current events arouse your interest? Or would you much rather be doing something else with your everyday leisure time? When Thomas Jefferson, who so inspiringly emphasized our human commonality as individuals, proudly declared, "I cannot live without books," was he also speaking on behalf of people like you? Or, perhaps in this case, mainly for himself? The Big 12 trait known as Intellectualism is last to be highlighted, but it often plays an important role in intimate relationships. Too often, however, it has been overlooked or ignored altogether as a personality feature that often brings people in love closer together or drives them further apart. It's surprising, but true.

Some men and women seek intellectual stimulation as a

wonderful pleasure, wholly valid on its own terms and requiring no wider justification. Indeed, it may be completely unrelated to their work, career goals, or personal lifestyle. Reading, studying, and researching are acutely enjoyable for them, just as listening to a new song, wearing a chic new jacket, or skiing down a slope may be.

People high on Intellectualism aren't necessarily scientists or professors, journalists, writers, or legal or industrial researchers. But just try taking away their morning newspaper, Internet access, or favorite news program, and you'll have a huge battle on your hands. Others, of exactly the same mental ability or IQ, have no such attraction to or interest in these things at all. They may be diligent and up-to-date in their work skills and knowledge — and even quite successful in terms of promotions and salary — but have absolutely no desire to learn about subjects outside their field of specialization; you won't find them dabbling in history or popular science, listening to news shows, attending public lectures, and generally keeping abreast of global events.

The crucial point here isn't that we differ in our cognitive abilities or problem-solving preferences, such as verbal versus mechanical or social versus spatial. While certainly relevant to education and job training, they're secondary matters when it comes to the realm of intimacy. Rather, the issue is that because of differences in levels of Intellectualism as a core trait, some of us readily embrace Helen Keller's statement, "Books are my utopia," whereas others reject it as almost incomprehensible. Depending on where two people stand on this issue, greater harmony or discord can result.

EARLY SIGNS

Despite what's sometimes advertised on the radio, you can't teach a toddler to read, even with the latest "breakthroughs in phonics."

But often by kindergarten, boys and girls high on Intellectualism show a keen interest in books — and by elementary school in specific subjects like science, history, and current events. Such youngsters are not always academic-contest winners, and they may not even rank at the top of their class. But they are avid readers and enjoy discussing the news and speculating about the future: They get "high on ideas." Sometimes tormented by peers in early adolescence and called "bookworms" and "eggheads," typically by high school they accept their intellectual bent, especially if they have acquired some friends with a similar inclination. They're likely to attend a college emphasizing academic achievement rather than a reputation for socializing or partying.

When does this all begin? Believe it or not, we begin hypothesizing about the world very early on. And once we form these notions, we then test them: "Is this different from what I have previously encountered?" We then rapidly categorize the world into like and unlike patterns, sets, events, and experiences. Contrary to what psychologists once believed, it's now clear that infants have the ability to abstract, average, and represent information preverbally. But what makes one child more interested in reading and thinking than another? As yet, that remains a mystery.

BEYOND STEREOTYPES

It's long been a popular image perpetuated by TV and movies that those high on Intellectualism are emotionally distant and sensually frigid — concerned only with their test tubes, microscopes, or ultramodern computers. Comedies, love stories, and horror films all capitalize on this theme. But no evidence exists to support this view. Rather, people who enjoy reading, discussing ideas, and keeping up with current events are just as likely as others to be emotionally warm and libidinous.

SELF-QUIZ ON INTELLECTUALISM

Please read each question carefully and mark the one answer that best fits you. There are no right or wrong answers, and you need not be an "expert" to take this quiz. Describe yourself honestly and state your opinions as accurately as possible. Be sure to answer each item. If you make a mistake or change your mind, erase your answer completely. Then mark the number that corresponds to your correct answer.

- Mark a 1 next to the statement if it's *definitely false* or if you *strongly disagree.*
- Mark a 2 next to the statement if it's *mostly false* or if you *disagree.*
- Mark a 3 next to the statement if it's *about equally true or false,* if you cannot decide, or if you are *neutral* on the statement.
- Mark a 4 next to the statement if it's *mostly true* or if you *agree.*
- Mark a 5 next to the statement if it's *definitely true* or if you *strongly agree.*

_____ 1. In school, I was teased for being a "bookworm."
_____ 2. I can't stand working with eggheads.
_____ 3. Libraries bore me.
_____ 4. I avoid listening to panels and debates on TV or radio.
_____ 5. I enjoy talking about current events.
_____ 6. I like browsing in bookstores.

_____ 7. People who use big words when they talk disgust me.

_____ 8. I must admit I read little.

_____ 9. I am fascinated by history.

_____ 10. I can't imagine wasting my time by doing research on the Internet.

_____ 11. I like to discuss trends involving marriage, love, and family life.

_____ 12. I listen to books on tape while driving my car.

_____ 13. Intellectual people turn me off.

_____ 14. I think about how the world will be in the future.

_____ 15. Reading has never been a source of pleasure for me.

_____ 16. If I go to a bookstore, it's just to use the café.

_____ 17. I would avoid spending an evening with people who talk about ideas.

_____ 18. It's fascinating to do research on the Internet.

_____ 19. People who read a lot are interesting to me.

_____ 20. I enjoy going to libraries.

_____ 21. I typically read at least one book a week.

_____ 22. Listening to lectures on the radio puts me to sleep.

DETERMINING YOUR SCORE

- Add the numbers you wrote by these statements: 1, 5, 6, 9, 11, 12, 14, 18, 19, 20, and 21.

    Total for part A_____

- Now subtract the numbers by these statements: 2, 3, 4, 7, 8, 10, 13, 15, 16, 17, and 22.

    Total for part B_____

Your score on Intellectualism is A minus B:_____.

INTERPRETING YOUR SCORE

Scores on this self-test of Intellectualism can range from −44 to +44.

If you scored 22 or more, then you are *high* on Intellectualism. You enjoy reading, talking about ideas, and thinking about current events and future trends. Society and history interest you. Browsing a bookstore or library, doing research on the Internet, or listening to a lecture are likely all turn-ons to you. You're filled with admiration for thinkers, writers, and those who focus on the mental world. It's probable that activities such as learning a new language pique your curiosity. Your soul is fed by shared intellectual experiences with a loved one.

If you scored 21 or less, then you are *low* on Intellectualism. The bookish world just doesn't excite you. While you may certainly respect those who speculate about ideas or analyze trends, such activity definitely isn't your cup of tea. You almost invariably find it foreign and even dull. Academics, and indeed all attracted to the ivory tower, strike you as boring. You get true gratification from other sorts of endeavors. And you'll gain intimacy from these rather than from shared Intellectualism.

INTELLECTUALISM: THE FOUR SCENARIOS

YOU BOTH SCORE HIGH

Take a few bows, you two. You deserve it. In a society that shows little interest in cultivating new ideas, delving into history, or pondering the future, you've each found a partner who shares a trait that is so important to your happiness and fulfillment. This is no simple accomplishment, as you both undoubtedly know. Indeed, we'd be willing to lay odds on the fact that when you were younger you were teased and called names like "book-worm" and "egghead" and that you fretted about such name-calling. Eventually, of course, you found like-minded friends in college, and now be glad, for you have one as your romantic partner as well.

At home, you'll often enjoy sitting beside each other absorbed in a good book, magazine article, or news item. Discussing such material will give you both considerable satisfaction — particularly the sense that your partner isn't just politely listening but is carefully considering your opinions. It's being taken seriously that gives you fulfillment.

As a couple, you'll find yourself choosing like-minded friends who share your strong intellectual bent. You may attend public lectures and seminars, or prefer salons and dinner parties with a more casual atmosphere. Whether formal or relaxed, it's the presentation of new ideas that will stimulate both of you. Of course, expect to spend many pleasurable hours together leisurely browsing in bookstores or searching the Internet for interesting sites.

BELIEVE IT OR NOT...

- If your partner is high on Intellectualism, she quickly feels starved for conversation about ideas or current events. People-talk is not her main course. Abstractions and ideas are the ultimate turn-on.

- If your partner is low on Intellectualism, he gets lost when swamped with ideas. What is of interest to him is small talk about people, things, and events. He does this with enthusiasm and pride with regard to subjects he knows well.

Your greatest challenge? To cherish your mutually high compatibility on Intellectualism while still valuing and growing through activities in other spheres of life. Stereotypes about the "bookish" being dull still abound, so if you can both learn a few good jokes about postmodernist philosophy, you've got it made.

YOU BOTH SCORE LOW

Living in the proverbial ivory tower has never appealed to you two. When it comes to focusing on what's important day to day, you know it's certainly not books. Typically dry, outdated, and just plain irrelevant, literature gives neither of you much pleasure in comparison to many other activities. Each of you has doubtlessly felt this way since childhood. Individually and as a couple, you take justifiable pride in dealing with life practically,

focusing on what's important in the present. Dwelling on the past has never seemed sensible to you. Rehashing history endlessly — analyzing absurdly trivial details (does anyone really care what Abraham Lincoln and his wife had for dinner the evening he was shot?) and speculating fruitlessly about what might have happened if something different had occurred (suppose Lincoln had stayed home that night

> ### IF YOU FIND YOURSELF THINKING...
>
> - *Doesn't my partner ever read a book?*
>   You're involved with someone low on Intellectualism.
> - *Does my partner always have to be buried in a book?*
>   You're involved with someone high on Intellectualism.

with a stomachache and never been assassinated: What then?) — just leaves you cold. If one thing is sure, it's that we can't change the past.

Ditto for endless future-gazing. Wanting to predict the stock market certainly makes sense, and it would be great to know next year's World Series winner and defeated foe. But who really loses sleep about projected high school literacy trends in Asia over the next twenty years or unmanned space exploration plans among the European Union? Science fiction movies may occasionally be entertaining, but people who take all that futuristic stuff seriously in today's busy world really have too much free time on their hands.

As a pair, you'll embrace friends who view life the same way: realistically and without escaping into the rarified atmosphere of ideas. If you read a daily paper beyond the front page headlines, it's likely that financial news, movies, sports — and of course, relevant advertising — spark your greatest interest. Let others ponder Australia's cutback in urban renewal, upcoming elections in France, or wetlands research in Bangladesh. Life is too short and interesting for you two to get worked up about such matters.

> **GREAT EXPECTATIONS**
>
> - If your partner is high on Intellectualism, expect to hear about current events, science, or history.
> - If your partner is low on Intellectualism, don't expect frequent visits to bookstores and libraries.

Your greatest challenge? To peek sometimes into the garden of new insights that lies beyond your practical routine. For you each may be cultivating ideas and plans that can enrich your activities together. Welcome this garden too into your life, and you'll have a combo that can't be beat!

You Score High, but Your Partner Scores Low

Be prepared to spend a lot of time reading, learning, and speculating about life with minimal interest from your partner. Did you just finish a fascinating political analysis in today's paper? How about a stimulating new biography or a book about upcoming genetic breakthroughs in curing illness? On the drive home this afternoon, did you hear a fascinating foreign author interviewed on public radio? Regardless of the specific venue, it's likely that you'll be experiencing such intellectual pleasures alone. Pure and simple, your partner finds such matters totally boring.

> **WHAT YOUR PARTNER LIKES TO HEAR**
>
> • If he or she is high on Intellectualism, ask, "Did you read anything interesting in today's newspaper?"

Don't expect much company, either, during your avid bookstore browsing. Your partner may obligingly head for the café to imbibe a latte and then make a quick tour of the magazine rack. But soon enough, you'll find yourself pleading for a few minutes — and then just a few more after that — so that you can happily, even dreamily, peruse the store's beckoning aisles.

You may find yourself wondering if there's a particular new book available that might arouse your partner's reading interest, but deep down you know you're whistling in the proverbial dark. Seeing him or her get really excited over a book, or a magazine or newspaper article for that matter, is about as likely as seeing a nearsighted librarian portrayed as a superhero in this summer's blockbuster.

Likewise, if you're fortunate enough to receive frequent invitations to salons or parties where current events, culture, and new ideas are discussed, don't count on enthusiasm from your partner. He or she may grudgingly attend but really perceives such events as pretentious as well as tedious. In your partner's view, what do such intellectual get-togethers really accomplish or produce but a lot of hot air? "Get a life" might well be the unspoken message you each harbor for the other.

You Score Low, but Your Partner Scores High

"Books are good enough in their own way, but they are a mighty bloodless substitute for life," declared Robert Louis Stevenson more than a century ago. It may initially seem odd that the celebrated author of *Treasure Island, Kidnapped,* and other adventure novels expressed this harsh sentiment. But Stevenson saw decisive action, not thinking, as the core of a meaningful existence — and you would heartily agree that avid reading is ultimately a blind alley. Unfortunately, you're paired with someone who has minimal inkling of what Stevenson's cogent outlook is all about.

Expect to be bored often by your partner's constant talk about what he or she just read in the newspaper, or in a magazine, in a book, or on the Internet. In some ways, you'll feel that you're trapped by a news junkie, relentlessly and uncaringly subjecting you to the dull and trivial almost every day. You suspect your partner of showing off his or her up-to-the-minute awareness of the world, but also, in truth, of avoiding real, practical aspects of daily living.

WHAT RUFFLES YOUR PARTNER'S FEATHERS

- If your partner is high on Intellectualism, he gets ruffled when deprived of reading or conversation about current events.
- If your partner is low on Intellectualism, she gets ruffled when expected to talk about books or world trends.

Whether you're taking a road trip, shopping in the super-market, even swimming or playing golf, your partner will virtually never take a breather from this obsession with news, not to mention with history, science, or future social trends. Get used to it, for this situation is not going to change. Indeed, even on vacation, you may find yourself badgered into stopping at a bookstore. At your favorite resort, you may be inescapably exposed to mind-numbing factoids about foreign economies or disappearing animal species that your partner finds endlessly fascinating. No matter how

EXPRESSING AFFECTION: GIFT-GIVING AND COMPLIMENTS

When your partner is high on Intellectualism:
- Give her a book or journal to write in.
- Compliment his knowledge of current events, history, or science.

often you reply, "Who cares?" either gently or forcefully, the barrage will continue. It's easy to be tempted by the fantasy that one glorious day your partner will look up from his or her tedious magazine article and announce, "I've had it with all this reading. I apologize for all the times I've bored you. It's time for me to get a life." But the more you indulge in this fantasy, the more you are denying the discord in your relationship. When an old Chinese proverb compared a book to a "garden carried in the pocket," it conveniently forgot to mention the weeds.

PART THREE

FINDING YOUR SOULMATE

CHAPTER SIXTEEN

CREATING YOUR COMPATIBILITY PROFILE

B y now you've undoubtedly gained a clear perspective on the Big 12 traits that underlie romantic compatibility. You've tested yourself on each of these vital qualities that affect all relationships. If you have a partner, you've either invited him or her to take these quizzes or guessed his or her likely answers. If single, you have gained a valuable perspective in your romantic search. Now it's time to construct your Compatibility Profile, the vital culmination of what you've learned about yourself and your partner in the previous chapters. As should be evident, everyone, regardless of age, gender, background, or nationality can be effectively rated on each of the Big 12. It's an easy process of discovery, involving seven steps that will guide you. When you're finished, you'll have a clear picture of where you stand on these important qualities that affect intimacy.

YOUR INTIMACY PROFILE

STEP 1

After you have completed all twelve quizzes, mark your scores
on chart one below.

CHART ONE		
TRAIT	SCORE	FUNCTIONING LEVEL (HIGH OR LOW)
1. Need for Companionship		
2. Idealism		
3. Emotional Intensity		
4. Spontaneity		
5. Libido		
6. Nurturance		
7. Materialism		
8. Extroversion		
9. Aestheticism		
10. Activity Level		
11. Subjective Well-Being		
12. Intellectualism		

STEP 2

Using chart one as your basis, now organize your scores using the following summary chart.

CHART TWO	
I SCORED HIGH ON THE FOLLOWING BIG 12 TRAITS	I SCORED LOW ON THE FOLLOWING BIG 12 TRAITS
1.	1.
2.	2.
3.	3.
4.	4.
5.	5.
6.	6.
7.	7.
8.	8.
9.	9.
10.	10.
11.	11.
12.	12.

YOUR PARTNER'S INTIMACY PROFILE

STEP 3

After your partner has completed all twelve quizzes, mark his or her scores on chart three below.

CHART THREE		
TRAIT	SCORE	FUNCTIONING LEVEL (HIGH OR LOW)
1. Need for Companionship		
2. Idealism		
3. Emotional Intensity		
4. Spontaneity		
5. Libido		
6. Nurturance		
7. Materialism		
8. Extroversion		
9. Aestheticism		
10. Activity Level		
11. Subjective Well-Being		
12. Intellectualism		

STEP 4

Using chart three as your basis, now organize your partner's scores using the following summary chart.

CHART FOUR	
MY PARTNER SCORED HIGH ON THE FOLLOWING BIG 12 TRAITS	MY PARTNER SCORED LOW ON THE FOLLOWING BIG 12 TRAITS
1.	1.
2.	2.
3.	3.
4.	4.
5.	5.
6.	6.
7.	7.
8.	8.
9.	9.
10.	10.
11.	11.
12.	12.

STEP 5

Now that you have constructed your Intimacy Profile, as well as your partner's, it's time to compare your scores. This step helps you create your Compatibility Profile.

YOUR COMPATIBILITY PROFILE

CHART FIVE		
TRAIT	YOUR LEVEL (HIGH OR LOW)	YOUR PARTNER'S LEVEL (HIGH OR LOW)
1. Need for Companionship		
2. Idealism		
3. Emotional Intensity		
4. Spontaneity		
5. Libido		
6. Nurturance		
7. Materialism		
8. Extroversion		
9. Aestheticism		
10. Activity Level		
11. Subjective Well-Being		
12. Intellectualism		

STEP 6

Using chart five as your basis, now form your Compatibility Profile Summary Chart.

Your Compatibility Profile Summary Chart

High Compatibility

My partner and I are compatible (either high/high or low/low) on the following traits:

1. _____
2. _____
3. _____
4. _____
5. _____
6. _____
7. _____
8. _____
9. _____
10. _____
11. _____
12. _____

Low Compatibility

My partner and I are discrepant (either high/low or low/high) on the following Big 12 traits:

1. _____
2. _____
3. _____
4. _____
5. _____
6. _____
7. _____
8. _____
9. _____
10. _____
11. _____
12. _____

Uncovering Your "Must-Have" Compatibility

The more you match your partner on each of the Big 12 traits, the greater your joy together. This is absolutely so. But as we've seen in our combined forty years of psychological experience, it's rare to find happy couples who are in sync on every single trait, or even on all but one or two.

Isn't this a paradox? Not really, for sharing something psychologically related is definitely crucial to a lasting bond. What do we mean? Simply this: that every individual cherishes some of the Big 12 qualities above others for personal well-being, especially when it comes to intimacy. If you think about this notion for a moment, it makes perfect sense. For example, reading an interesting news article might certainly be stimulating for Sally, who is high on Intellectualism, but has much less impact on how happy she feels when listening to her favorite CD or working out after a stressful workday, meaning she scores higher on Aestheticism and Activity Level. Conversely, Jason, who is high on Spontaneity, is truthful when revealing how much he'd like to go somewhere exotically adventurous — but when it comes to most weekends, his high Extroversion propels him into loud parties, however familiar the place and people.

When it comes to our intimacy needs, this reality is even more compelling. Deep down, we all know what personality compatibilities must be present in a love relationship for us to feel validated, joyful, and alive. Indeed, when thinking about their former boyfriends or girlfriends, most people easily pinpoint the specific discrepancies — such as those involving Libido, Idealism, or Need for Companionship — that caused the relationship to falter or end.

Soon we will help you uncover what you consider to be your four "must-have" traits for intimacy. Over the years, we have found repeatedly that when couples match on *three or more* of their four "must-have" traits, their bond is deep and satisfying, no matter how many years pass. However, if they match on only *two or fewer* of their primary-need traits, their relationship is much less likely to be mutually fulfilling.

Looking now at your Intimacy Profile, be completely honest with yourself. Identify which four traits among the Big 12 are truly vital for your happiness in an intimate relationship. To facilitate this important self-examination, which nobody else can perform for you, we've developed two helpful exercises. You may wish to do these exercises at two different times.

1. First, put yourself into a relaxed, meditative frame of mind. Now go down your personal Intimacy Profile slowly and notice

your gut reaction to this question concerning each trait: "Suppose it were suddenly taken from your personality for the rest of your life? How would you feel?"

For instance, if you scored low on Activity Level, what's your reaction to imagining that you could never relax comfortably on your couch again? Or if you scored high on Aestheticism, how would you feel if you could no longer enjoy music, art, or film? When you look inward in this way, which four traits evoke the strongest response as essential to your well-being?

2. Imagine that each of your twelve scores is abruptly and permanently turned into its opposite. For each trait, how painful is this to contemplate? For instance, if you score high on Emotional Intensity, what's your reaction to the image of yourself as having mild, placid feelings about virtually everything for the rest of your life? Or if you're low on Materialism, how do you feel about being transformed into someone greatly interested in what's chic and fashionable?

When you have finished reviewing your Intimacy Profile, identify a specific trait that ranks as a "must-have" for love happiness. For example: high on Need for Companionship or low on Spontaneity.

Next, select a second of the remaining eleven traits.

Now select a third of the remaining ten traits.

Finally, select a fourth of the remaining nine traits.

STEP 1: MY "MUST-HAVE" TRAITS FOR INTIMACY

1. _____

2. _____

3. _____

4. _____

Look over the list again, making any appropriate changes. There are eight remaining traits. Of these, which four emerge as your "second-tier" list? Mark these now on the lines provided below.

STEP 2: MY SECOND-TIER TRAITS FOR INTIMACY

5. _____
6. _____
7. _____
8. _____

STEP 3: MY THIRD-TIER TRAITS FOR INTIMACY

Owing to the process of elimination, only four traits now remain. Certainly though they may have significance for you in everyday life, be aware that they carry less weight than the other traits in terms of happiness and validation in love. Note them in the lines provided below.

9. _____
10. _____
11. _____
12. _____

STEP 4: YOUR PARTNER'S "MUST-HAVE" TRAITS FOR INTIMACY

Now ask your partner to do the same process, based on his or her own Intimacy Profile. Or, as objectively as possible, decide what your partner's four most likely "must-have" traits would be. If you are currently single, go directly to chapter 17.

1. _____
2. _____
3. _____
4. _____

Step 5: Your Partner's Second-Tier Traits for Intimacy

Have your partner look over the list again, making any appropriate changes. There are eight remaining traits. Of these, which four emerge for your partner as having "second-tier" importance? Mark these now on the lines provided below.

5. _____
6. _____
7. _____
8. _____

Step 6: Your Partner's Third-Tier Traits for Intimacy

Owing to the process of elimination, four traits remain for your partner. Mark these now on the lines provided below.

9. _____
10. _____
11. _____
12. _____

Step 7: Your "Must-Have" Compatibility Profile

You have now determined your four most important Big 12 qualities for lasting intimacy and those of your partner as well. How many were matches, and which traits did these involve? Are you delighted or relieved by what you see? Or do you feel disappointed? Look at your second-tier and third-tier clusters, and make a similar comparison.

In the final chapter, we'll see what all this really means.

IF YOU OFTEN
HEAR YOUR PARTNER SAYING ...

1. I just read an interesting news article. Do you want to hear about it? *That's a sign he's high on Intellectualism.*

2. There's an interesting new art exhibition. Let's go see it on Saturday, okay? *That's a sign she's high on Aestheticism.*

3. I've got nothing fashionable to wear for going out this weekend. I need to go shopping, pronto. *That's a sign he's high on Materialism.*

4. There's a sexy new movie with my favorite star. Let's go see it, okay? *That's a sign she's high on Libido.*

5. This party is really getting loud! I'm so glad we came! *That's a sign he's high on Extroversion.*

6. What a cute baby! I'd love to snuggle her in my arms. *That's a sign she's high on Nurturance.*

7. We've got to make changes in our society to help the poor and homeless. *That's a sign he's high on Idealism.*

8. I just had a great idea: let's go out now to that new restaurant and cancel our other evening plans, okay? *That's a sign she's high on Spontaneity.*

9. I don't want to just sit at home tonight and do nothing. *That's a sign he's high on Activity Level.*

10. I had a dream last night that I'd like to tell you about. *That's a sign she's high on Need for Companionship.*

11. I feel like crying after seeing that tragic news story on television. *That's a sign he's high on Emotional Intensity.*

12. Everything will be fine! Don't worry! *That's a sign she's high on Subjective Well-Being.*

CHAPTER SEVENTEEN

WHERE DO YOU

GO FROM HERE?

N ow you have read the book and taken the quizzes. You have drawn up your Intimacy Profile, and either your partner has done the same or you have done it for him or her, allowing you to determine your Compatibility Profile. If you have taken the quizzes in your partner's stead, you have used your feelings, perceptions, and experiences as your guides. This process is still highly accurate. For if this is how you interpret your partner, then this is your reality. As we see every day in our therapeutic practices, a person's subjective view of life has huge significance. If you are currently not involved with anyone, then you have taken the quizzes in an effort to sensitize you to who you are and what needs are arising from your constellation of traits. Knowledge is power and it is now yours to use as a tool to find a compatible partner.

However you have done it, now that you've drawn up your Compatibility Profiles, let's see what they look like. There are three possible conclusions you may draw from these profiles. Let's examine them in order: high, low, and in-between compatibility.

HIGH COMPATIBILITY

And now for the headline: You and your partner have received the glorious news of big-time compatibility! Congratulations! You have chosen your four "must-have" intimacy qualities, and you have checked your partner's ratings — and glory be — you are a wonderful match.

This is not to say that you'll never have tension in your relationship. How could it be otherwise? No one is a clone of the other. But it does mean that your partner knows your essence, shares your most valued interests, and can give you what you want and need. Your soulmate has the tool kit for making you happy. Yours is a match made in heaven.

Bob and Rachel are an example of a happy match. They met at college and attended the same graduate school. When they were finished, they decided to marry. For along with the physical attraction they felt for each other, both had the calling to serve. What and whom they wanted to serve was not yet clear. Besides being high on Idealism, both were low on Materialism and felt that continuing to live in the United States in an upper-middle-class lifestyle wasn't really for them. As a result, they relocated to a third world country. Divesting themselves of many of their clothes, the couple packed lightly and went abroad.

Life in their new chosen country was fierce. Fighting broke out nearby, often too close for comfort. Rachel, the more susceptible one, became ill. Some natives mocked them, calling them "foreigners, invaders, infidels." But working with children, educating, and providing parenting and counseling filled Bob and Rachel with joy and a sense of deeply felt commitment to their beliefs. Despite their travails, the often-unbearable heat, and the always-present potential of falling ill, they stayed.

Sometimes there were tensions between them. When Rachel became very ill, Bob feared for her life. She could see the pain in his eyes each time he touched her fevered brow. He wanted them to leave. But he, with the same worldview as she, became convinced through her pleas that she was young, strong, and doing what she felt in her heart she had to do.

Both were also high on Subjective Well-Being: They were natural optimists. Emotions play a large part in our life. Feeling optimistic, Rachel used this energy to get better. And so they stayed. Because they were similar in so many ways, they also could negotiate. About once a year, they would come back to the States to see family and friends. Both high on Intellectualism, they enjoyed studying their new country's language and became fluent in it. This helped them become more accepted, and they started to develop friendships with the native population.

High on the trait of Emotional Intensity, they both felt deeply about life and what it had to offer. They were also very compatible on two other traits: Need for Companionship and Extroversion. Both were high on the first and low on the second. Thus, together in a foreign country, they needed and loved being together rather than with large groups of people. Alone with each other, each could and did bare their souls, taking pleasure in sharing small, intimate details of each day. Revealing, they knew, made them feel more as one.

Here is another story. Ken and Samantha are both high on

Need for Companionship. Though they have only been married for two years, they are very tight. They love being with one another and sharing their dreams, hopes, and plans for the future. A beautiful, lavish home and shopping together are also essential to them, both being high on Materialism. When Samantha shops for clothes, Ken sits and watches her try everything on, steeped in admiration. When he shops, Samantha is the cooing mother. They are in sync, two birds in one nest. Their marriage may be on earth, but its heart and soul are in heaven.

Both high on Extroversion and low on Activity Level, they enjoy dinner parties with mutual friends once or twice a week. Sometimes there's a video and other times just lots of delightful food and beverage. They laugh about being proud "couch potatoes" and about the unused exercise equipment they received as a wedding present, gathering dust in the basement. Both come from large families and enjoy entertaining at home their many out-of-town relatives. Like Bob and Rachel, they share compatibility on all four of their "must-have" traits for lasting intimacy.

What can you do with your own good fortune? See it as a gift from above. Treasure it. Be grateful that these scores — the evidence of who you and your partner are — confirm that out of this vast sea of humanity you have found your perfect match. And, if you believe in a Higher Power, know that your meeting did not happen by chance. If you're not a believer, accept your intimate bond for what it is: a miracle, no matter how you interpret it.

This acceptance will plunge you deeper and deeper into your relationship. Secure in the knowledge that it is good, live this goodness. Don't hold back. Don't be afraid of giving your all. Take the risk of experiencing unfettered joy with your beloved. Be aware of what you possess. Hug it to your breast, and take pleasure in recognizing that you and your partner have a harmonious, in-sync relationship. The Compatibility Profile gave you your scores. But a tool is only as good as its user. Use your new knowledge; it can only bring you good. And, as actress Mae West once quipped, "Too much of a good thing is a good thing!"

LOW COMPATIBILITY

It came as no surprise to you, for the symptoms were always there: the fighting over large and small things, the lack of interest, the desire for a real friendship that never seemed to unfold, the awareness that relationship and happiness should go together but somehow did not. You knew in your gut that something was wrong but did not know what.

And so you pointed the finger outward: to money. If only you had more, all would be well. Or it was the kids. If only you or your spouse weren't so busy with them, life could run more smoothly. Or perhaps it was your parents or your in-laws. If only they were not getting older and needing so much attention, life could flow like the nearby stream. Perhaps you sought help from therapists, like many other couples under stress. And the therapists tried to help. They were certainly well trained; you noticed all the impressive diplomas on the walls. And they were kind and compassionate. They empathically reached out to you, and you responded with gratitude.

But the pain, the turmoil, the gut feelings did not go away. You didn't know where to look or what to do, a quandary none of us likes to be in. If only someone would push you and tell you to leave, give you permission, insist that you are wasting your life, maybe you could do it. You waited for a real change to come, a magic wand to appear and wave all the pain away. But it never did.

Now you have looked at your scores and realized that every-thing that seemed wrong in your relationship is due to low compatibility. If you don't share your "must-have" traits for intimacy, there is no meeting ground. You are a cello and your partner is a trumpet. Of course, there is nothing wrong with either of these instruments; both produce beautiful music. But how can the cello listen to the trumpet and respond like a trumpet? And vice versa. If you are not compatible, you may be speaking the same language but not really hearing the other. Indeed, you have more in common emotionally with a foreigner who does not speak your language but who is compatible on the traits most important to you.

Margaret and Henry married young and then had two daughters. Said Margaret, "I knew right after the honeymoon that it was not going to work, but I wanted to give it a shot. We eventually tried therapy. Nothing changed. We had the kids, but when I thought of spending the rest of my life with him — since we seemed to have almost nothing in common — my soul grew dark. But, typical of many women, I stayed for twelve years, then decided on divorce. Henry was a nice man — no abuse, no affairs, no drinking — but there it was: nothing. When I told my best friend, Dorie, who lived next door, that I was getting a divorce, she said: 'But we never hear you yelling at each other.'

"True. But if we didn't yell, it's because there was nothing to yell about, since there was no mutuality of interests. It was the loneliest feeling in the world: living with a stranger. We were polite to each other but even sexually we were worlds apart. Spiritually too. I believe in God. Henry used to sneer and insist I was neurotic, that he could never be a believer. He was also distrustful of people and would constantly say I was just naive, that one day I would see the world as it really is: cold and heartless. A chill went through me whenever he said this. I knew that if I stayed, I would feel entombed. Deep down, I knew he felt the same. I left. Although Henry didn't say so, I think he was just as relieved as I. We could now be free to find who we needed, and who needed us."

Perhaps you know couples like Margaret and Henry. Having determined your scores, you now know that you and your partner are in a similar boat. It's a simple truth: You realize you are truly two different people. Neither of you is good or bad, right or wrong, holier than the other — just different.

As humans, we see and make choices. And sometimes these choices are right for us, and sometimes they are wrong. Yet it can be hard to leave, even when the facts are in. Why? For one thing, many of us, women in particular, feel that if we just stay awhile longer, try a little harder, all will end in love. While it's fine to be optimistic, from our long-term experience, this kind of dream never materializes. Here's something to ask yourself: Was it ever good? How good? If it wasn't, it is never going to be, no matter how much you try. Another question to ask yourself is, Was your relationship ever alive? Or did it start off in a coma and then just die?

You may think, as you have been told a thousand times by movies, novels, plays, operas, and all those around you that "love will win out." So you have tried and tried. But such unconditional love is only applicable in parent-child relationships. If your toddler does something you disapprove of, you don't throw him out of your house. You pick him up and hold him, explaining that you love him but reject his behavior. And then, most important, you teach him what he must change. But a love relationship is not between an adult and toddler. It is between equals. And so, as an adult, you have a choice to make. Rather than obsessing about all the dead-end "what ifs," now that you actually see where the discrepancies lie, you can take action. If your relationship has not been good for a long time, or even a painfully short one, chances are that you have already left your partner many times in your mind. Or you may have asserted, "I've had it. This is it. I'm leaving. Only a fool/idiot/slave would stay any longer."

But you have not left. The fear of aloneness, the lack of trust in your ability to connect with someone new, the anxiety over unknowns are keeping you a slave. This scenario is reminiscent of the childcare worker who, alerted to neglect or abuse, attempts to remove the child from the home and find a replacement. Paradoxically, but typically, the child clings to the parents, and screams and pleads: "Don't make me go! Please, I want to stay!"

How is this situation possible? It's simple: habit and familiarity. The parental neglect or abuse is known, and even predictable. Familiar demons are always preferable to those unknown. But you, an adult, can make conscious choices: an ability we humans are blessed with. You can take action, be in charge of your life. Give yourself a gift. Trust. Know that if you know what you want, you can get it. There is a Higher Power waiting to give to you. Ask for it. You will be responded to. As for your partner's changing, a person who's entered adulthood takes with him or her all the qualities they were born with. The older we get, the more we become who we are. A rose becomes more roselike, a gardenia more like a gardenia.

Recognize that love is a feeling, a movement toward as well as away from someone. This feeling sensitizes you, alerting you to the actions to take. All feelings are survival mechanisms, given to us so that we can take appropriate action. If we see

someone menacing approaching, we feel fear and remove ourselves. The opposite is also true: If someone loving approaches
us, we draw nearer. Examine your feelings now that your score-
card is in. They are probably skewed toward those termed the
"negative emotions," though, in truth, all emotions are to be honored for their innate purpose: survival. Feelings do not lie. If you
have experienced mostly depression, unworthiness, anxiety, fear,
disappointment, sleeplessness, over- or undereating, heed your
body's message and do something about it. Your mind, heart, and
soul will decisively benefit. To wait and wait in misery is merely
"waiting for Godot" as the title of Samuel Beckett's play suggests.
Trust and do what you need to. All life is to be lived!

THE GRAY ZONE

When the day is filled with dazzling sunlight so bright it hurts
your eyes to look up, it is clear: This is a bright, glorious day.
Conversely, when you peek outside your window and see dark-
ened skies and hear distant rumblings, you know what's ahead.

But what if the day is somewhere in between? What if it's
light gray, and there's a slightly overcast sky, but threads of
golden sun are slipping in between the clouds? Should you dress
for rain or stride outside expecting the warmth of the sun to
embrace you? From our experience, this scenario is the hardest.
Here you are not in a black-or-white situation. Rather, you stand
in that in-between place, the gray zone. There's enough good to
keep you from leaving, but as Shakespeare said, "and here's the
rub," enough bad things to make you want to leave. What should
you do? Should you stay or go? This inner tug-of-war is among
the most difficult of human conditions. Your strongest emotions, perhaps even your deepest sense of what kind of person

you are, are pulling you in different directions, and you're in pain. But remember, you did not come to this situation overnight. It has to have been there for quite a while. Although it has made you very uncomfortable — as with all of life's messages, there is a reason for it.

Now you have to act. Don't blame yourself. That only drains your energy and leaves you confused, listless, and depressed. Give yourself permission to have experienced what you needed to in seeking love. Only then will you be able to think clearly and leave or stay as you wish. If, of the four qualities most important for you in intimacy, your partner shares three, maybe you ought to stay. But if it's two or less, the house is empty — there's nobody home.

To make all this more concrete, close your eyes and feel what it was like when it was good. Slide into the feeling. Stay. Place yourself in some "good-times" scenarios and steep yourself in them. Now do the same with the bad times.

Sense what your body, mind, and soul are telling you. United, they are your messengers. Acknowledge them. Pay homage to them. They are present to help you live your life the way it was meant to be. Still listening to your inner feelings, identify the point at which the good tips over into the bad. As you do, you will discover the particular compatible personality traits at the root of your conflict. You may be surprised which way you will go.

Let's look at an example of one way to go: Paul and Cara had been married for five years. It was his second marriage, her first. Paul had a son of eight when they married who lived with them. Paul was high on Activity Level. With a large inheritance from his father, money was free. And he wanted to spend it all on his favorite activities: ice skating, tennis, rock climbing, canoeing in exotic countries, getting a black belt in martial arts, and traveling, traveling, traveling. His son was delighted.

But low on Activity Level, Cara was distraught, especially after recently becoming pregnant. This was a conflict on one of her four "must-have" qualities. Nesting was important for her happiness. She loved reading quietly on the couch, watching TV, or doing crossword puzzles. She wanted a home, a hearth with a fireplace and the security of a close-knit family. These things felt confining to Paul, and they argued constantly. But there were compensations. Cara could spend whatever she wished, for Paul was generous. If she came home with a pair of $800 Italian shoes, his comment was, "You should have bought three pairs!" Paul was sincere, and Cara was appreciative. Yet Materialism was not on her priority list.

One of Cara's "must-have" traits was Libido, and on this they were well matched. Both delighted in sexuality, and the touching, holding, and kissing that accompanied it. Cara's only complaint was that if he were not around, she had no partner for lovemaking.

But on Cara's "must-have" trait of Aestheticism, a big gap existed. She greatly enjoyed music, poetry, and art. Yet when, on her insistence, Paul accompanied her to the opera, he fell asleep and snored so loudly that they had to leave. Though apologetic, Paul said he could not fathom what she saw in opera. The language was foreign, and besides, everyone died at the end. What was the point of it all? Cara didn't laugh at this. She knew that if she wanted to go to the opera or an art exhibition, she would have to go by herself or with a friend.

They did share compatibility on another Big 12 trait besides Libido that Cara considered vital: They were both low on Spontaneity. Cara and Paul delighted in scheduling their days and weeks in detail and took pleasure in forging an organized, predictable life. Their favorite vacations were well planned and invariably involved familiar locales.

Cara decided to stay, knowing that she and Paul were compatible on only two of her four "must-have" qualities for intimacy. She understood there was little, if any, chance that Paul would change. He was who he was. And she was who she was. The bottom line for her was that he would provide well for her and their child. That was her conscious choice. You also need to know your bottom line, remembering not to expect major changes in your partner.

The truth is that there is no generic, one-size-fits-all Prince Charming. Even in the classic fairy tale, the prince who rescues poor Cinderella from her evil stepmother and toxic stepsisters has a set of specific — and identifiable — personality traits. For the sake of illustration, and to have some fun, let's examine these: 1) He was high on Emotional Intensity. He felt deeply upon first meeting Cinderella at the ball, taking time off from his princely duties to go seeking for her. 2) He was high on Activity Level, going from house to house, one slipper dangling from his hand, to find his lady — lots of energy expended there. 3) He had to be high on Extroversion, because in seeking her out, he encountered and turned away many mothers eagerly thrusting their daughters at him. And, 4) most obviously, he was high on Libido, the undercurrent of his quest all along.

As for his bride-to-be, let's look at what Cinderella was all about: 1) She was certainly high on Activity Level, working at marathon speed, scrubbing, cooking, cleaning for the cruel family she lived with, even if these were not the activities she desired. 2) Where did she rank on Emotional Intensity? Well, she felt deeply about the wonder of life, or else she would have been unreceptive to the Fairy Godmother's magic. 3) How about Libido? She was obviously hot for the prince. And 4) she had to be high on Extroversion. Cinderella certainly lacked banqueting experience, yet she did well at the ball, mingling comfortably with everyone. How else could the cinder-girl transform herself into a party-girl in one night?

This seven-hundred-year-old fairy tale of Prince Charming and his swept-off-the-feet bride who live happily ever after, at its core, still resonates today. If you find a potential soulmate who has at least three of your four "must-have" Big 12 traits, and four to six of the other eight, hang in there. Your path is clear. Good luck!

YOUR SOULMATE
IS OUT THERE

B y now, we hope you've gotten the message. There is no one-size-fits-all soulmate. That view is as outdated as believing that the sun revolves around the earth. Prince Charming and Aphrodite not only have bodily functions like all the rest of us human beings, they also have their own core personalities — and Intimacy Profiles — involving the Big 12. How do you find your soulmate? Here is Richard's story. A songwriter and conductor, he joined the Music Lovers Society. His first date was with a pediatrician, Karen. After deciding how to identify themselves, they agreed to meet at the opera box office, and each found the other attractive. They went inside and had a terrific time. Each knew the operatic score, played several instruments, and enjoyed talking about various performers and recordings. So far, so good!

Then Richard suggested they have a light dinner at a new Indian restaurant. Karen liked the idea but was annoyed that he had forgotten its name and exact address; she prided herself on being well organized. They began to walk. As Karen talked about her life goals, she noticed Richard's lack of interest. Suddenly, she slid on the ice and scraped her knee. Richard made no effort to comfort her and complained that his former girlfriend had made demands on him after breaking her leg in a skiing accident last year. Karen couldn't believe that he didn't even ask to look at her bruise.

As for Richard, he disliked hearing her self-disclosures, and as they walked and window-shopped, he was disinterested in her talk about fashionable clothes and sunglasses. Karen could see that he was bored with the entire subject.

Once they were at the restaurant, Karen opened up about her childhood, career, and plans. Richard was again unresponsive. He kept turning the conversation back to music, and wondered why Karen was revealing such private things. Moreover, nothing seemed to animate him. Even before the check arrived, Karen mentioned that she had to get up early the following morning and had enjoyed the opera with Richard. They politely shook hands. Then each went home disappointed.

But wait, the story has a happy ending — at least for our friend Richard. On his second date via the Music Lovers Society, he met Amanda, who was a music teacher and also played the violin professionally. Amanda was dressed in a department-store pantsuit with no jewelry. After the opera, she suggested they eat in a new Italian restaurant, and when she confessed that she had forgotten its name and exact address, they both laughed and stopped instead at a diner.

Over coffee and danish, Amanda discussed how she had

recently played the violin at a church concert for homeless families. Richard, who had often played the piano as a volunteer in nursing homes, was filled with admiration. He was particularly absorbed as Amanda described the logistical problems of busing the children into the concert from diverse neighborhoods.

Like Richard, Amanda considered herself a private person who felt little need to bare her soul to anyone. She almost never divulged her dreams or hopes in life. Not once did she mention her childhood or ask Richard about his. She was so glad he never once asked her to name her "favorite movie of all time" or "three things you'd want to take if stranded on a desert island" or other mildly self-revealing questions about herself.

Each was a soulmate on the other's four "must-have" qualities: high on Aestheticism, high on Idealism, low on Materialism, and low on Need for Companionship. Because of such matching, each went home delighted, telling their friends about their excellent date. Within a year, they had married and have enjoyed a happy bond for fourteen years.

Are they compatible on all of the Big 12? No. As for the other eight, they differ on three: Amanda is higher than Richard on both Nurturance and Emotional Intensity, and lower on Subjective Well-Being. Do they argue at times? Of course. Are they living happily ever after? In our real world, a definite yes!

Each fulfills the other's four "must-have" traits and matches on five of the other eight. And, not surprisingly to us, each considers the other a soulmate. In fact, we asked Richard and Amanda that question each independently just last week.

We don't know what happened to Karen. But we hope she has been equally successful. We hope that on her second date, she met a music lover who shared her three other "must-have" qualities besides Aestheticism. Maybe it was Dan, a human resources manager at a large corporation who had likewise recently joined the Music Lovers Society. And maybe this occurred:

When they met at the opera house, Dan was wearing expensive clothes. Karen was pleased about that. Later that evening, they enjoyed looking at fancy jewelry in the windows on Fifth Avenue when Karen again slipped on the ice (no, it wasn't a ploy to check out her dates — it was those high-heeled shoes). Dan gently hugged her with concern and insisted on examining the wound.

Over cappuccinos at an elegant café whose name and address Dan knew precisely, they chatted knowledgeably about the opera. Like Karen, Dan had played several instruments since childhood and loved music. Then, after a pause in the conversation, Dan opened up immediately about his aunt's recent death from cancer and how angry he had been about her poor nursing care. Dan told Karen how much he had loved his aunt and how sad he had felt when the inevitable arrived.

Then Dan asked if she ever cried when a patient died. Karen was stunned. None of the men she had dated in the past year and a half had directly asked her this, and certainly not on a first date.

Much to Karen's surprise, she became tearful as she recounted a fourteen-year-old girl's death from meningitis during her first month of pediatric residency. She talked about how helpless and angry she had been that the girl's parents had waited five days before taking her to the emergency room, where she was immediately placed in intensive care and where she died the next evening.

Dan spontaneously took Karen's hand, listening closely. And then she noticed tears in his eyes too. Neither talked about music as the hours passed, but about their careers, hopes, and dreams in life, often laughing loudly together. Finally the café closed at 2:00 A.M. They spontaneously hugged, and each went home excited.

When Dan called the next evening, the first thing he asked was about Karen's bruise. They met for dinner later that same week, and are now engaged to be married — clearly sharing their four "must-have" traits among the Big 12: they are both high on Aestheticism, high on Need for Companionship, high on Emotional Intensity, and low on Spontaneity; they match on six of the remaining eight traits.

If we could ask Karen and Dan, we suspect that each would consider the other a soulmate.

Do these scenarios sound too good to be true? They're not! True compatibility in love is possible for you too. Having discovered this, you now have your work cut out for you. When you know who you are and what you need, it's time to act. You can feel blessed if you are in a highly compatible relationship, leave if you definitely are not, and decide what to do if you're somewhere in between. Don't delay. Be your own best friend. Give yourself the advice and support you need, and move on. If one thing is sure, it's that this carousel will never come around again. You only get out of life what you put into it. Put your energy into doing something for yourself, and it will come back at you in newfound happiness, deeper if you're already there and revealing its fresh beauty to you if you're a novice. Most of all, your new discoveries will be the golden threads of wisdom for you to use in weaving the rest of your life.

Regardless of your prior experiences or your age, you have charted a new beginning. We wish you a glorious bon voyage!

REFERENCES

Bergmann, Martin S. *The Anatomy of Loving.* New York: Columbia University Press, 1987.

Carey, William, and Sean McDevitt. *Coping with Children's Temperament: A Guide for Professionals.* New York: Basic Books, 1995.

Chess, Stella, and Alexander Thomas. *Temperament: Theory and Practice.* New York: Brunner/Mazel, 1996.

Cohen, David B. *Strangers in the Nest: Do Parents Really Shape Their Child's Personality, Intelligence, or Character?* New York: Wiley, 1999.

Costa, Paul T., and Robert R. McCrae. *Bibliography for the Revised NEO Personality Inventory (NEO PI-R) and NEO Five-Factor Inventory (NEO-FFI).* Odessa, Fla.: Psychological Assessment Resources, 1994.

Digman, John M. "Personality Structure: Emergence of the Five-Factor Model." *Annual Review of Psychology* 41 (1990): 417–40.

Epstein, Gerald. *Healing Visualizations.* New York: Bantam, 1989.

Forrest, Linda. "Career Assessment for Couples." *Journal of Employment Counseling* 31, no. 4 (December 1994): 168–88.

Goldberg, Lewis R. "The Structure of Personality Traits." *American Psychologist* 48, no. 1 (January 1993): 26–34.

Goleman, Daniel. *Emotional Intelligence.* New York: Bantam, 1995.

Hendrick, Susan. *Close Relationships: What Couple Therapists Can Learn.* Pacific Grove, Calif.: Brooks/Cole, 1995.

Hoffman, Edward. *Psychological Testing at Work.* New York: McGraw-Hill, 2001.

———. *Ace the Corporate Personality Test.* New York: McGraw-Hill, 2000.

———. *The Right to Be Human: A Biography of Abraham Maslow.* New York: McGraw-Hill, 1999.

———, ed. *Future Visions: The Unpublished Papers of Abraham Maslow.* Thousand Oaks, Calif.: Sage, 1996.

Hough, Leatta M. "The Millennium for Personality Psychology: New Horizons or Good Old Daze." *Applied Psychology: An International Review* 47, no. 2 (1997): 233–61.

Jeannert, Richard, and Rob Silzer, eds. *Individual Psychological Assessment.* San Francisco: Jossey-Bass, 1998.

Kagan, Jerome. *Galen's Prophecy: Temperament in Human Nature.* New York: Basic Books, 1994.

Kroeger, Otto, and Janet Thuesen. *Type Talk at Work: How the 16 Personality Types Determine Your Success on the Job.* New York: Dell, 1992.

Labovitz, Shoni. *God, Sex and Women of the Bible.* New York: Simon & Schuster, 1998.

Lichtheim, Miriam. *Ancient Egyptian Literature: A Book of Readings.* Berkeley, Calif.: University of California Press, 1975.

Lutz, Tom. *Crying: The Natural and Cultural History of Tears.* New York: Norton, 1999.

Mitchell, Stephen. *The Enlightened Heart.* New York: Harper & Row, 1989.

Molfese, Dennis L., and Victoria J. Molfese, eds. *Temperament and Personality Across the Life Span.* Mahwah, N.J.: Erlbaum, 2000.

Murstein, Bernard. *Love, Sex and Marriage through the Ages.* New York: Springer, 1974.

Piedmont, Ralph L. *The Revised NEO Personality Inventory: Clinical and Research Applications.* New York: Plenum, 1998.

Plutchik, Robert. *Emotions in the Practice of Psychotherapy.* Washington, D.C.: American Psychological Association Press, 2000.

———. *The Psychology and Biology of Emotions.* New York: HarperCollins, 1994.

Richardson, Peter Tufts. *Four Spiritualities: Expressions of Self, Expressions of Spirit.* Palo Alto, Calif.: Davies-Black, 1996.

Sarthes, T. "Ambivalence, Passion, and Love." *Journal of American Pyschoanalytic Association* 25 (1977): 53.

Schopenhauer, Arthur. "The Metaphysics of Sexual Love." In *The World as Will and Representation*, edited by E.F.J. Payne. New York: Dover, 1966.

Singer, Daniel, and Marcella Bakur Weiner. *The Sacred Portable Now.* Rocklin, Calif.: Prima, 1997.

St. John, Warren. "Young, Single and Dating at Hyperspeed." *New York Times*, 21 April 2002, sec. 9, pp. 1–2.

Stahmann, Robert F., and William J. Heibert. *Premarital and Remarital Counseling: the Professional's Handbook.* San Francisco: Jossey-Bass, 1997.

Starr, Bernard D., and Marcella Bakur Weiner. *The Starr-Weiner*

Report on Sex and Sexuality in the Mature Years. New York: Stein and Day, 1981.

Strelau, Jan. *Temperament: A Psychological Perspective.* New York: Plenum, 1998.

Thomson, Lenore. *Personality Type: An Owner's Manual.* Boston: Shambhala, 1998.

Thorman, George. *Marriage Counseling Handbook: A Guide to Practice.* Springfield, Ill.: Thomas, 1996.

Tieger, Paul D., and Barbara-Barron Tieger. *Do What You Are: Discover the Perfect Career for You through the Secrets of Personality Type.* Boston: Little, Brown, 1995.

Van Duzen, Grace. *The Book of Grace: A Cosmic View of the Bible.* Loveland, Colo.: Eden Valley Press, 2001.

Weiner, Marcella Bakur, and Armand DiMele. *Repairing Your Marriage After His Affair: A Woman's Guide to Hope and Healing.* Rocklin, Calif.: Prima, 1998.

Weiner, Marcella Bakur, and Bernard Starr. *Stalemates: The Truth about Extra-Marital Affairs.* Far Hills, N.J.: New Horizon, 1991.

————. *The Starr-Weiner Report on Sex and Sexuality in the Mature Years.* New York: Mc-Graw Hill, 1982.

White, Marjorie T. and Marcella Bakur Weiner. *The Theory and Practice of Self-Psychology.* New York: Brunner/Mazel, 1986.

INDEX

ABOUT
THE AUTHORS

EDWARD HOFFMAN, PH.D.: A licensed clinical psychologist in New York City for the past eighteen years, he received his B.A. from Cornell University and his masters' degrees and doctorate from the University of Michigan. Dr. Hoffman has authored numerous books, including several award-winning biographies and two on personality testing He lectures widely in the United States and abroad on topics related to personal growth and enhancing creativity. His books have been translated into Chinese, French, German, Japanese, Korean, and Spanish.

Photo Credit: Lou Manna

MARCELLA BAKUR WEINER, PH.D.: A Fellow of the American Psychological Association (APA), Marcella Bakur Weiner is also an adjunct professor of psychology at Marymount Manhattan College in New York City and president of the Mapleton-Midwood Community Mental Health Center, a

treatment center for community-living residents. Prior to her current pursuits, she served as senior research scientist for the New York State Department of Mental Hygiene where she published seventy articles. On faculty for the Institute for Human Relations Laboratory Training, Dr. Weiner has trained professionals in the United States and in countries overseas, including China, Japan, Cuba, Switzerland, Norway, Denmark, Sweden, Panama, Thailand, Greece, Turkey, Egypt, and Israel. Dr. Weiner is the author of and contributor to twenty books.

Photo Credit: Lou Manna

New World Library is dedicated to publishing books,
audiocassettes, and videotapes that inspire
and challenge us to improve the quality
of our lives and our world.

Our books and tapes are available
in bookstores everywhere.
For a catalog of our complete library
of fine books and cassettes, contact:

New World Library
14 Pamaron Way
Novato, CA 94949

Phone: (415) 884-2100
Fax: (415) 884-2199
Or call toll-free (800) 972-6657
Catalog requests: Ext. 50
Ordering: Ext. 52

E-mail: escort@nwlib.com
www.newworldlibrary.com